LOVE

In gratitude for *Love* . . .

It is hard for me to imagine that anyone could feel more gratitude than I do. I am grateful to my husband, Donald Deeb, for his recognition of the changes in me and for his telling me about them and naming for me the essence of those changes. Like the night he told me I was more at ease and, because I was more at ease, the whole family was more at ease. Like the night he told my dad he couldn't remember the last time we had a fight. Or the night he simply told me I was good. I am thankful that while I didn't voice what was happening, he recognized it anyway and, in his own way, joined me in making love and grace and peace real in our lives.

For both Julie and me, having our husbands read the *Love* manuscript was a necessary part of sharing our experiences with them. And although both of us feared that sharing, it only proved to us once again that sharing conquers fear. We each extend our gratitude, to both Donny and Kelly, for their acceptance of our story and their willingness to be part of the whole that continued unfolding with the publishing process.

Each family member and friend who read *Love* blessed me with acceptance. Telling this story was like "coming out of the closet" for me. I could not tell anyone what had happened. I had to write it and let them read it. I can't begin to express the relief I felt when each person *Love* was given to gave love in return. Those I most feared judgment from were those whose support was the

IN GRATITUDE

strongest and loveliest, especially that of my mother, Madeline Diprima Perron. Sara Cole and Shirley Koski, Mary's and Julie's mothers, were the other early readers whose acceptance gave us the strength and courage to go on. Then came the encouragement of Deb Bohnen and Jeff Heggem, two people whose words of praise meant more to us than I can convey.

The list of readers went on from there . . . to siblings Susan Lucio, Mike Perron, John Perron, Ray DiPrima, Liz Cole-Degroot, Charlie Cole. To friends . . . Lou Crain, Sally Austin, Deb Kelly. To co-workers Felicia Christy and Sheila Riley. It seemed that each one held our lives in their hands as they read our story. We thank each one for treating them with dignity.

A special thanks, as well, to Vernon Weckwerth for support of another kind but support that was always steadfast.

The Hazelden team became part of the miracle of *The Grace Trilogy*, beginning with Dan Odegard's vision and understanding of the truly real and continuing through each step of the process and with each person involved.

Love's editor, Caryn Pernu, often guided me to where deeper meaning already existed within the text but was hidden between the lines. With a gentleness that was greatly appreciated, she nudged "more" from me even when I didn't think I had more to give.

Although *Love* is almost a prayer of gratitude for my spirit sisters, I note here again how thankful I am for them.

AN ACKNOWLEDGMENT

If every writer doesn't have a faithful "first" reader of her work, she should have. *Faithful* is the operative word. Without the inexhaustible faith that my friend and reader Ann Mulally Reilly has had in me and my writing, I may not have given up, but my progress would have been greatly delayed. A first reader's faith is a miraculous thing—balm for the soul, inspiration for the muse, it buoys the spirit. A writer's faith in her first reader is also amazing. When Ann told me that *Love* was the best writing I ever did, her words were as powerful to me as those of Maxwell Perkins might have been to a writer of a few decades ago. It is not only because Ann likes my writing that I have always found her to be a woman of impeccable character. That is just the way she is. And to have as a first reader a friend whose honesty is never in doubt, who is innocent of judgment, and who loves the written word is the finest combination that could possibly exist. Ann is one of the many blessings in my life for which I am truly grateful.

INTRODUCTION

HOW IT BEGAN

This is a story about the chance encounters that come together and give form to a life, about the impact one life has upon another, about being affected. This is a story, in its most basic form, about friendship. It is about seeing the patterns of chance in the lives of three friends as more than chance. Like the beauty that reveals itself on a slow walk through the woods on a sunny day, the paths, the choices, the obstacles, and the adventures of our journey stood out, clear and simple and lovely and rare. It is a story of observance. As if life stood still while we captured it, saw what it was, and eventually came to write it down.

It was on December 19, 1995, that we decided to tell this story. It wasn't chance that this decision was made at my kitchen table over a conversation with my friend Mary Love. It was simply the culmination of events that had made up our year, made up our friendship.

We began not necessarily as friends but as co-workers. I had worked with another woman, Julieanne Carver, for an off-site adult-study program at the University of Minnesota for several years before we hired Mary. Julie and I thought of our positions as high-stress because we worked for a biostatistician considered to be an eccentric genius, because our program did not "fit" the university's usual mode of operation (making our day-to-day functioning more difficult than was necessary), and because we had adult students on campus throughout the summer. We had just lost a beloved co-worker who was bright and funny and, more important, mischievous and irreverent to job burnout, and we needed to replace a person we considered irreplaceable.

We wanted someone we would get along with, someone whose skills would complement ours, but we wanted more than that too. Julie thought we should hire someone with university experience; she sought the security of known skills—someone familiar with the bureaucracy

2

and forms of the university, familiar with computers and budgets. I thought we should hire someone who had been in a professional career, someone with the less definable skills of knowing how to maneuver in any environment in a professional manner. I sought someone who would possess qualities that were important to me, qualities that I was trying to develop in myself. So did Julie. But skills and professionalism were only a small part of what we were hoping to develop. The larger part fit in the "something more" category and those qualities were like seedlings ready to sprout. They hadn't quite broken the surface yet so that we could identify them. But they were there.

Despite not knowing what it was I truly sought, I realized almost immediately that I knew someone who would be perfect for the job and who also would provide the "more" that Julie and I were looking for. That someone was Mary Love. How I knew Mary Love would be the perfect complement to me and Julie I do not know. But I knew.

I had met Mary only once before she came to interview with Julie and me. She was the daughter of my mother's best friend, Sara, and she had invited my mother, sister, and me to lunch one Christmas. It was one of those polite social gatherings one attends during the holiday season without much enthusiasm. Everyone is busy. Another luncheon on the calendar at Christmas had about as much appeal as a trip to the dentist. I had things to do!

3

But I also had a "thing" about my mother. After years of being in conflict we had made our peace, and I was eager not only to keep it but to build upon it. Her friend Sara seemed a bit of a bridge in that regard, as Sara genuinely liked me in a way I had never really thought my mother had. For years Sara had been reeling off a list of the things we have in common—a fondness for poppy seeds, being Aquarians, and a love of reading—in that way people have of associating themselves with those they admire. If there was any appeal to the luncheon for me, it was the thought of basking in the glow of that admiration.

To my surprise, Sara's admiration seemed to have passed to her daughter Mary as well. She had heard about me, she said, and thought how interesting I sounded. What attracted Mary, in addition to the similarities I shared with her mother, was that I was a writer, a title I was just beginning to feel I had the right to claim, as I had recently completed my first book.

The luncheon was a success, something I've come to believe could happen on Mary's charm alone. She is a warm, sweet-faced, soft-looking person with an animated way of talking that includes much laughter and hand gestures. We are about the same age, height, and weight, neither of us overly pretty or separated by any of those things that tend to separate women: a disproportion of intelligence, education, money, looks. Although she had no children of her own and I had three, she was recently married and had a stepdaughter. Our husbands were of a similar

4

type, obvious from the beginning as we laughed over the reason Mary had almost called off her wedding: her husband's collection of empty plastic yogurt containers he hadn't wanted to part with when they set up residence together. Two men who were savers were something that two women who were not could immediately identify with. But there were other things, about our husbands and about our careers, both of which had veered in the direction of health care for no particular reason. The "liking each other" bond was sealed, however, when Mary produced a seventy-year-old scrapbook she and her husband had purchased at an estate sale. It was the keepsake of a woman named Claire, simple mementos of an ordinary life, tenderly kept, and on that pre-Christmas afternoon four years ago, tenderly shared.

Thus began the connection that brought Mary to my kitchen table and before that to my place of employment. At the time of the luncheon, Mary had taken a six-month leave from her job and was looking for a change. When the job opening presented itself at my office, I sent her the relevant information and she began the tedious process of applying for a university job.

Luckily, she had the right background, the right talents. She was available and I knew she would work hard. But I would have expected anyone we considered for the job to have certain talents, to work hard. It wasn't what I wanted in a co-worker. What I wanted was something more. Something more, even, than professional competence.

When pushed to define it further, I labeled it a warm and outgoing personality that would balance the quieter, more introverted personalities of Julie and myself. But it was more than that too.

At the holiday luncheon, Mary had revealed not a professional self, but a very human self. The part of Mary that had touched me as we laughed over yogurt containers and almost cried over Claire was what I was really looking for. This part of Mary that was a treasure. The Mary who could share her humanness in such a simple yet profound manner. Yet I wasn't ready—then—to admit to that longing to be touched, to connect.

Julie had not had the benefit of seeing Mary's humanness exposed at a holiday lunch, but Mary's humanness was as easily recognized during an interview as at a social event. If I had any doubts they were erased when Vernon, our director, was introduced to Mary. He asked Mary not about her skills, but about her birth order. Mary announced, raising her right hand as if to take an oath, that she was a firstborn, identifying proudly with the firstborn qualities of perfectionism and leadership. He grunted. Seeing that this answer had not been accepted with favor, Mary quickly launched into how she was really like a secondborn because her brother, who had been born just a year behind her, had been sickly. "Charlie got all the attention," Mary said. "I learned to fend for myself." If Vernon didn't want perfectionism and leadership, she'd give him independence.

Yes, I knew it. Mary was the one. Julie knew it too. We offered Mary the job and she accepted.

Mary's joining us was the beginning of the story, the beginning of seeing those chance encounters of life as something more than chance. And from the beginning, there was a feeling that Mary belonged. But it was more than that. It was more that the three of us belonged together in that time and in that place and that Mary Love was to be the tie that bound us, the loop that completed our circle.

Almost from day one we realized that we were together for a reason. But that reason did not reveal itself immediately. For a while we simply worked. Mary had a job to learn; we had programs to run.

We worked in a rather schizoid department where we did everything from the most tedious clerical duties to traveling around the country promoting the program at professional conferences. I, in an effort to get Mary to accept the job, had emphasized its professional nature. It was almost with embarrassment that I listened during Mary's interview while Julie asked how Mary felt about doing mailings.

Mary's job was a twin, or perhaps I should say a triplet, of my own. Mary, Julie, and I each ran separate portions of one program. We each separately admitted students, but jointly prepared their curricula. We each separately scheduled faculty, but jointly prepared a master schedule. We each were in charge of separate events, but all would attend them and assist each other in making sure they ran smoothly. The three positions had to work in concert with one another. We were a team on which having the right skills and personalities was paramount.

I was told once that I could administer a small Third World country. Being a good administrator is a dubious skill, something akin to being seen as an excellent bureaucrat. But still, it was the main attribute I brought to the group. Good at planning and meetings and seeing the big picture, I filled a role that needed to be filled. I was also seen as the communicator, which was equally true, at least in writing. I had less confidence in my ability to promote the program through person-to-person encounters. I did not see myself as warm or outgoing.

I did not see Julie that way either. Julie's unique skill was an ability with numbers and an orientation to detail that had often kept other office workers from making costly or embarrassing mistakes. She often said the important thing was to get things done right, not just to get them done. In the two years we had worked together before Mary's arrival, Julie and I had not developed a personal relationship. She was younger by a decade, tiny in stature, one of those women who, although not from money, looked as if she were. Quiet and dignified, she was a person you could count on to get to work on time, leave on time, and not produce any creative breakthroughs or dreadful mistakes while she was there. In short, she was also one of those people you need to have on a team, and we had been good teammates; we just had too little in common and were both too quiet and reserved to become friends.

We needed Mary.

Almost immediately, Mary did what I somehow knew she would do. She began to transcend the label of "co-worker" and become "friend." And what's more, what she began transcended our individual boundaries. Everyone in the office became better friends.

With the blossoming of these friendships came an appreciation for Mary, the change agent. Mary stories became legend. We retold the story of her interview and meeting with Vernon time and time again. Mary would say, as we sat down to a 2,000-person mailing, "I didn't know what you meant when you asked how I felt about mailings," and we would laugh and talk again, for the tenth, the fifteenth time, about how Mary came to work with us. Even my teaching her to use the computer became story material. As she learned, she would wield the mouse with the sweeping strokes of an orchestra conductor, often traveling off the mouse pad and to the edge of the desk and then exclaiming, "Oopsie! Oopsie!"

Because of its humanness, this story became part of the fabric of our lives. Before Mary, we had not told stories. Our day-to-day existence had not inspired the immediate remembrance, the oral tradition, that working with Mary inspired. It was almost as if from the beginning we were continually recognizing and reinforcing the rightness of our decision, the pleasure that had come from it, the joy Mary was adding to our lives, the feeling that Mary was meant to be with us.

And yet our work lives were still ordinary. We went through six months together before any major changes occurred. And it was a good six months. Julie and Mary got along better than I had ever thought they would and there arose, at times, the difficulties inherent in the number three. The rules every mother knows are true—two kids play well together and three are trouble. We were adults, of course, and we weren't playing, but the trouble came and went and the team functioned as well or better than it ever had.

Mary had been hired in April and it was November when the news came. Not a one of us at work would ever forget it. We had a long, narrow office with the receptionist's desk right inside the door. The desk was our gathering place for morning conversation before the workday began. It had before it one of those modules with a shelf on top. In winter, especially, it invited the laying down of purses and gloves while one took off one's coat and deposited it on the other side of the door at the coat rack.

Mary's hair was cut short and it gave her face a pixieish quality. On this morning, the color in her cheeks was particularly high, her hair (which she changed often) was a burnished red, her look one of pure radiance. I must have just come in myself because I was there to see the entrance. It seems to me in retrospect that everyone was appropriately gathered around. Mary hadn't even taken her coat off when she swept her eyes through the group, slammed her purse down on the shelf, and announced, "I'm pregnant." We would tease her about this later because she had planned to wait three months to tell us and had been unable to wait three minutes.

Julie immediately got tears in her eyes. "Congratulations," she said. Mary could see that the tears were not only tears of joy but tears that reflected Julie's own disappointment. For she had been trying, thus far unsuccessfully, for a second child. As is apt to happen in an office of women, all of our menstrual cycles had grown to be close together and Mary asked, "Have you gotten your period yet this month?"

Julie shook her head and Mary announced that she had the second half of her two-try home pregnancy kit with her. The two scurried off to the bathroom. The remaining nonpregnant among us quickly toted up the months. One baby, possibly two, would be due in July, at our busiest time of the year.

Within a week we had two confirmed pregnancies with due dates three days apart. The bond between Mary and Julie was sealed. While I was happy for them both, I also knew that they would share something I could not. I felt as if I was doomed to be odd woman out in the threesome, the one who would be left to get us through our busy season with no experienced team members. I

11

felt a little jealous of the closeness they would share. That closeness began immediately.

From the first days of being joyous and beaming, through the months of being tired and squeamish, and on to the early days of wearing maternity clothes and feeling the first faint movements of life, they relied on each other for comfort, support, and encouragement. Julie, having already had a child, could say, "Oh, it's normal to feel that way," or, "I feel that way too." Once a month we took Polaroid snapshots of their ever-increasing shapes and mounted them side-by-side on office walls. We guessed at who would have a boy and who would have a girl. We discussed the merits of one name and another. They talked of doctor visits, the thrill of hearing their babies' heartbeats, the coming labor and delivery. They dreamed of how their children would be friends and teased that they would grow up and marry.

As summer approached I planned the shower. With Mary's mother and my mother being best friends, I decided to give a shower with a mother-daughter theme. Mary's mother-in-law drove up from Madison, Wisconsin; her mother and mine had an excuse to celebrate together; all of us co-workers had the chance to meet the other mothers we had heard so much about. I made a game of "momisms" in which the shower guests had to guess which of the moms regularly said things like, "That makes me so nervous," or "a lick and a polish." I threw in a few from the new mothers as well: Mary's

"I'm going to el baño," Julie's "I'm so tired." No one knew it would be one of the last joyous days of the pregnancies.

By early June we had been moved to smaller office quarters. Julie, Mary, and I were in one room and the remainder of the office staff was in another. No longer in private offices, our desks were separated by cubicle walls and we were so close together that if one of us sneezed the other two would immediately say, "God bless you."

So it was that when I received the call from a frantic Mary, Julie was at my desk within seconds. Mary was at her doctor's office, alone and in shock. She had been told that her baby had a malformation, later diagnosed as an arterial ventricle malformation, and that the prospects were not good.

It is hard to describe shock, or a sharing of a misery so deep and primal, but it was all there in Mary's voice, Julie's face as she heard the news. I worried for a time that we would have two babies affected, so deep and immediate was Julie's pain and heartsickness. She alone could imagine what Mary was feeling. All the fears of mothers everywhere converged in Mary's voice, in Julie's face. All the shared joys became reasons for doubt, suspicion, terror. "What if?" replaced happiness in that instant for both of them. For both it continued, sapping their energy. All things were in question.

For Mary, of course, it was reality. For the remaining few weeks of her pregnancy, the tests and the questions continued. *How bad would it be? Was there reason for hope?* The loss of control was complete. The body was no longer the trusted companion of life but the enemy, concealing secrets so devastating that it was obvious life would never be the same again. It was a great rift, a chasm that split life at its core. Mary plunged into it. Julie and I tumbled after her.

Julie gave birth to Peter on July 13, and he was robust and healthy. Little Grace was born on July 22 and lived five weeks. The paradox was complete. The fear, the questions, the "what ifs?" continued. What meaning is there in a hoax of such magnitude? All that was to be joy had become pain for one. The joy of another tempered by fear, by what if?

I wondered about the long-term effect. How, I wondered, could Mary come back—to life and to the team. I felt certain she would never be the same warm, outgoing person; certain she would never work with us again; certain that the pain of the happy memories of the shared pregnancies, and the pain of little Peter's reality, would be too much. I wondered how she would cope. How Julie would cope.

I had come close to losing a child myself during a difficult pregnancy, and the result of that almost-losing was a bond so strong it still gripped my heart, made it difficult for me ever to criticize or punish this child of my almost loss. This child who in her near loss became more precious than anything—than life itself. I felt I knew somewhat the bond Mary had developed with her daugh-

14

ter, Grace, as she struggled through the final days of her pregnancy, wondering how it would all turn out. My daughter had not been the longed-for child that Mary's daughter, Grace, had been, but when I almost lost her, she became my angel, later named Angela. She became the reason for my existence in the final weeks of my pregnancy. I felt as if I willed her to survive with the force of a love that grew more intense each day. I tried to imagine the pain Mary would experience in not being able to bring the bond of love she had developed with Grace into the future.

But I was wrong in thinking that the bond would not continue. The love, the bond, that had grown between Mary and Grace grabbed and held all of us. It followed us through our days. It changed our lives. There was a reason we were together, just as we had known from the very beginning. Only now we knew what that reason was. That reason was Grace.

I believe Grace happened at the right time—as Grace can only happen when the time is right. In other years, under other stars, the effects of Grace might not have been so apparent, so intense, so profound, so compelling. But I came to believe that Grace coming at the right time was all that was possible—that there was a divine plan at work in the universe.

I

ORDINARY WOMEN

P art of our reason for bringing this work to light was our belief, stated over and over again, that we are "ordinary" women. We would often say, If this can happen to three ordinary women, it can happen to anyone. What we, perhaps, meant by *ordinary*, was *familiar*. We are your neighbors, the women down the street, the ladies in the next office, the mothers at school conferences, the wives out for dinner with their husbands, the girlfriends out shopping, the devout of your church, the nameless women pushing shopping carts at the grocery store.

We are not, any of us, above average. We are average incarnate. We make less than $30,000 a year. We struggle with bills, with prioritizing, with children and husbands and in-laws. Two of us have been divorced. One has a husband with a disability. One has two children of mixed race. One's child died.

We are ordinary, average, and yet we are different. As each of you are different. We bring different hopes and fears and pains and joys to our friendship and to this collaboration. We have different failings and different gifts. We are three and we are one.

If we could tell you the limited range of our vision before this began. How little we saw of each other: We saw only the ordinary. Only the familiar. We saw what we chose to see, what the habits of a lifetime had led us to see. If only we could make you see that no one is ordinary, that in our ordinariness we are so much more.

It is hard now, even, to go back there, to that place where we were barely distinguishable from one another, and yet so different that we might never have met.

Mary eats so fast, she is done with lunch before Julie sits down. Julie brings a lunch of cheese sandwiches and animal crackers and a piece of fruit for weeks on end. I thought I was lazy. I was surprised when I found a message written at the bottom of my monthly vacation/sick-leave report that I had to start using my vacation time or I would lose it. I smoke and drink coffee and don't worry

17

about either. Mary has occasionally smoked, doesn't any longer, drinks coffee with cream. Julie partakes of neither and never has. Mary and I love to entertain. Julie would rather not. None of us has exercised this past year. We spend too much time talking at work and still get our work done. Mary and I have switched from drinking diet soda to regular and to drinking more juice and water. Julie never drank diet soda or ingested any NutraSweet. My children are almost grown, Julie's just beginning, Mary's stepdaughter in between. Our husbands guardedly like each other but are not friends. One works in heating and air-conditioning, one in alarm systems, and one is the owner of a guest residence. We are all college educated. We are all home owners. I have multiple vehicles (the teenagers), all American made; Mary two, Julie one, all foreign. I am the only one with a functioning garage. All of our husbands cook. Mary is Danish and English, Julie Norwegian, I a blend of Italian, Irish, and French-Canadian. We live in different cities on either side of the campus at which we work. Mary and I would be considered late baby boomers, Julie at the early end of Generation X. Mary is a firstborn, Julie a third, me a fourth. Mary is Sagittarian, Julie and I Aquarians. We all have eclectic tastes in music, but Mary has more jazz, Julie more U2, I more Jimmy Buffett. Julie and I were both born in the state in which we continue to live, Mary was not and spent her early years overseas. None of us is a hobby-ist. Two of us have cats (two each). Julie was a cheerleader,

Mary a homecoming queen candidate. I graduated from an alternative high school.

Although this barely scratches the surface of our differences and similarities, it is much of what we initially knew of one another. Much of what most people ever know about one another. It was nothing.

We came from a world in which work was important. Work was our bond and our goal. Work was where the drama of life played itself out. Who would lead and who would follow? Who would do this job and who that? Who would take vacation when? Who would supervise? Which of us would attract the most students to our program? Which of us would be better liked? How would we relate to our boss? How would we split, divide, distribute the workload into fair and manageable portions? How could we each contribute?

We came to work each day ready to do battle with the world. I can still remember Julie's face—she continues to wear it at times—when she would come in late. She had been the most dependable of employees: punctual, reliable, steady. Now, her two young children necessitated a woman who could be flexible. Who could do only what she could do within the confines of changing dirty pants, and finding shoes, and getting children strapped into car seats. This flexibility remains hard on her still, but not like it was then. It was all visible in her face, the defenses she had built to ward off the attack she was sure was coming: Why are you late?

I, too, was late. Sometimes I would arrive apologetic. Other times not. I thought, Julie at least has a good excuse. But she, because of day care, could not stay late to make it up. I could. I was one up on her.

Mary arrived, almost always pleasant. Warm. "I left my pain behind," her face, her voice, her posture all said. Before the baby as well as after, she came with her work persona: "I am fine. I am here to do my job. My personal problems are not here with me, thank you very much."

We all arrived hurried, breathless almost, from the effort of arriving. From the effort of leaving one world behind and entering another. From the transformation from one being to the next. Within the first half hour we were relieved. We had made it. We had arrived. The job would now occupy us. We would flow into its rhythm. We would chat, exchange information, interact. We would adjust our moods to the mood of the workplace. If it was busy, we rushed from one thing to the next, our rhythm staccato, our pace rapid. If it was slow, we would putter. Doing a little of this, a little of that. If the boss was visiting, we would stand up straighter, look busier, feel busier. If a co-worker watched the clock, we became slaves to time. If the secretary was not efficient enough, we wondered what to do. If all was going as dictated by our time line (an actual written document), we congratulated one another. If one person was busier than the next we made adjustments or held resentments. If two people seemed closer than the others, we closed ranks with those remaining. We drank our coffee, ate our bagels, went to lunch, had staff meetings and retreats. We prided ourselves on functioning well. We each fulfilled our duties. There is a reason such a place is referred to as a well-oiled machine.

What we had going for us was a boss who considered our work not a job but a mission, and one who hated bureaucracy. Thus, we were not rule bound, and, although the job was the bond and the goal, it was at least a worthy goal: education. Also, the nature of the programs we worked on, in which students came once a year to campus and became our charges, required teamwork and a social connectedness that went beyond the ordinary and usual.

The summer that the babies were born, at an after-work party in celebration of the end of our busy season, I shocked a student worker by having a few drinks and a good time. He said (after a few drinks himself), "But you're so rigid!" And I thought, *Me? Rigid?* How could this young man possibly have gotten this idea? Where? How? But there was no mystery to it at all. To him, I had become my work. I was only the person who demanded he be on time and responsible, and demanded more of myself: rigid. There I had been each day in my business suit, my work the most important thing in the world. Rigid. Part of me took it as a compliment.

But that was the summer I realized I had worked hard enough to take vacation. That was the summer of the

pregnancies. The summer it all began to break open. The
summer Mary's baby died. The summer that work was
suddenly not the most important thing in the world anymore.

It took a while to catch on. This breaking down of rigidity was like the dismantling of a wall, a fence, a brick
building. The wall of rigidity came down slowly. My
rigidity, I thought, was still my work. And my work was
my identity. It represented all I had "worked" so hard to
attain: a place in life, a title, a badge, a business suit,
respectability, a good reputation. It was my anchor.
Because the job was more than a job. It was also an
escape.

My full-time work life had begun when I was the single
mother of three young children. I now had a good husband, I owned my own home, and I had paid off every bill
that had accumulated over those years of trying to raise
children on my own. Yet this had not sunk in. Work was
still survival. Vacation was still something to be saved for
an emergency. A part of me still believed that work was
what kept me sane. There was a hidden undercurrent
that said as much as work was my life, it was also shielding me from a life that was even less controllable than the
one in the office.

For Mary, the rigidity was now pain. And work was as
much an anesthetic from that pain as television can be
from life. For a while, for those hours between eight and
five, the real could be replaced with the unreal. The pain

22

could be muted, if not forgotten. She could close the door on the home her child had never entered and drive away from the neighborhood in which her child would never run and play and in some way be held together by the rigidity of the workplace and the tasks to accomplish within the office walls.

For Julie, the rigidity was being the lucky one whose child had lived, whose child was perfect. But it was not always easy to be the lucky one who had to stay up all night with a sick child, change another dirty diaper just as she was ready to head out the door, the lucky one who had to pay someone else an exorbitant sum to take care of the children she would rather have taken care of herself. It was difficult to complain when you were the lucky one. For her, too, work was both a prison and an escape.

Identity, suffering, luck. For a while we tried to keep them all stuffed together, lumped into the overriding rigidity of work. The importance, the bond, the goal, of work. It gave us something to do. Something to hang our lives on. Something to fill our time. In a very real sense, it was our survival, monetarily and otherwise. How could it not be the most important thing in the world—at least for the eight to ten hours a day, five days a week we were involved in it?

And yet, how could it be? How simply silly, when seen in black and white, in the written form: Our goal, our bond, our importance, coming from our work. Our jobs. Simple jobs. Jobs that were not the stuff of brilliant careers. Jobs that were not our passions. Just jobs. Adequate, ordinary jobs. The jobs most people have. The earning-a-paycheck jobs. Jobs we were content with. Jobs we didn't want to lose. But still jobs.

Beneath the surface of our work lives ran the stream of our secret lives. Our secret selves. Out of one-dimensional life sprang dimensional life. We've spent the last year learning not to see just the surface but to delve beneath it. We have found treasures there.

We have found happiness in this pursuit. Out of the ashes life. Out of the darkness light. If it could happen to us it could happen to anyone. This is our message.

II

MOVEMENT

As ordinary women, Mary, Julie, and I were used to our lives proceeding in an orderly fashion, to having the kind of years difficult to discern from any other year. The unusual years were just that: unusual. We might remember the year we got married, be able to place our state of mind by remembering the years in which our children were born or some other major event took place. "Oh, yes, that was the year . . ."

We were, in other words, ordinary women expecting to

have ordinary lives. Some of us, more than others, thought we knew the direction our lives would take.

One of the reasons I had begun to get notices about my vacation building up was that I had been at the university for ten years. Ten years! Where had the time gone? I had not meant to be at the university that long but now that I had been I was thinking of retiring from the university. The first ten years had gone pretty fast, why not the next ten or twenty? As if years were something to be gotten through. And to be gotten through quickly.

Julie, as the youngest, was perhaps most open to possibilities. She thought of graduate school while her husband thought of expanding his business. Ten years into the future could very well mean incredible changes, life-altering changes. Just being the mother of young children made this so.

Mary had thought her life would go a certain way. That she would be raising a child for many years to come. That her life would be full of those child-rearing milestones, from yearly birthday parties to kindergarten and graduation. Her eight-year-old stepdaughter, Amanda, would still anchor her in these events for a little while. But the future loomed, undefinable.

I could dream of having books published and maybe not having to work for another ten or twenty years, but I had that ten or twenty years firmly planted in my mind. It was the most logical course of events. It comprised the most likely direction for my next two decades.

Encased in these various scenarios of the future, our ordinary lives went on. And they were full of not only scenes of the future but scenes from the past. The past seemed to abide in us, in our subconscious minds, keeping us company, a part of us.

There were childhood traumas from which we had not healed. Young-adult rebellions, that while necessary, had caused more harm than good. Grown-up mistakes that filled the mind with guilt.

We lived, as most people do, in part to build uncertain futures, in part to make up for unsatisfactory pasts, in part to survive the present. We were not only our work selves and our private selves, but also our selves of the past, present, and future. And these selves were seldom in accord. More often than not they were battling. The self of my past asked the self of my future by what audacity I could possibly believe I had anything to say that might be worthy of publication. I had made too many mistakes—too many wrong choices, from men, to education, to when to have children—to consider myself worthy. The self of Julie's past crippled her present with fears of abandonment and rejection. Her father's manic depression and parents' subsequent divorce had wounded something in her that had never healed. Mary's past called her to be a perfectionist, to not give anyone reason to criticize or ridicule her ever again. Having grown up wearing her heart and her ideas on her sleeve, she had suffered too much from that revelation to ever want to be revelatory again.

So we brought both our visions of the future and our beliefs from the past into the present with us. Both contributed to our unhappiness, to our ordinariness, to the surface images we projected and fought to be sure no one saw beneath.

We were basically stuck, though we did not know it . . . until Grace.

It is not, sometimes, until you stand back and review, that you see the rhythm and flow, the movement that has taken you where you have gotten. It wasn't until we began to look back, that the wonder of our journey filled us.

When we began to review, to think about telling our story, we thought it was essential to portray the fact that what happened to us was not something we went looking for. We did not join a movement or "get" religion. And yet, what our journey revealed was movement. The movement itself was the wonder of the journey. We were moving on . . . letting go of the past . . . moving forward. We had become our own movement. We had lived an unusual year.

And just as clearly, we realized that it was still going on. That it was not about to be *over*. That there was no over. For the story was still unfolding, as we were. As we are.

The story we tell here unfolded over the course of a year. But as you begin it, it is important for you to know that it continues. Important for you to know that it is not about getting "the answers," that it is not about winning

28

the lottery, that it is not about reaching a static place of wealth or success in which you feel you have made it and it is over. It is more about realizing that it is never over. That we are never anything but ordinary. That it is in our ordinariness that we are so much more.

The unfolding of the story took place over the course of a year. It began four months after Grace had died. It began, appropriately, in January.

I I I

WHAT WAS NORMAL?

By January of the year following Grace's death, life in our workplace had returned to a semblance of normality. The new calendar year arrived with all the attendant fanfare and resolutions. And, in our department, it was also the beginning of planning for a new academic year. There was a sense of the extraordinary wrapping up. Of the ordinary returning. We had experienced a crisis of both personal and professional proportions. We had survived it. It was time to get back to normal.

Mary, in keeping with the mood of the new year, planned a vacation. There was probably a collective sigh of relief at the news. Mary was putting things behind her, moving on.

Whether Mary felt this way or not, I did not know. It would have been intrusive to ask. But the vacation seemed to be a good sign—getting away, as it were.

Mary and her husband had planned a trip to Florida to visit his parents, to relax, to spend time sunning on the beach, to do whatever needed to be done to complete the healing. To get over it, some might have thought but never would have said.

But if it was to be a journey of forgetfulness, a New Year's journey of leaving the past and the pain behind, it did not work out that way. Instead it became the first time that Mary realized the pain would follow her wherever she went. The first time she realized she could not leave it at home, could not take a vacation from it. She could not drown it out in the wake of all the waves of the ocean. It was hers. It was her. It was.

Back at the office, the sound of Mary's tears reached across the miles to her friend Julie. What Julie heard was that it was not over. That it had only just begun. She stood in the office listening to a cry of loneliness she recognized. For she was lonely too. She stood outside my cubicle and said, "I think Mary is having a bad day."

Mary returned, leaving nothing behind. Returned with all she had brought with her. Julie asked, "Did you have a bad day last Wednesday?" Something had pierced the loneliness. For both of them.

"Yes," Mary said. "I did."

Mary had been on the beach crying. She cried as she looked out the car window while her husband, John, drove them to the beach. Sitting in the sand with John holding her, the wind blowing everywhere, she cried. Grief, as a friend of ours once said, is not compartmentalized like a jewelry box. It is a pool you get pushed into. And it includes all the grief you have ever experienced. It is all there waiting for you. All that was ever wounded is once again tender. You either heal it all or you don't heal at all. It is the archetypal choice between life and death. Mary hovered.

Her daughter, her Grace, had been born with an arterial ventricle malformation. What was God punishing her for? Her daughter, her Grace, had needed one surgery after another. What was God punishing her for? The surgeries permanently damaged the child who had been born with a hope, a chance of perfection. What was God punishing her for? She had watched her daughter, her Grace, suffer. What was God punishing her for? Her daughter, her Grace, slipped from life to death in the arms of her father while Mary was down the hall resting, absent. What was God punishing her for?

Life was not going to get back to normal. For what was normal about what had happened to Mary? What was normal about the death of a child only five weeks old?

What was normal? The grieving was clearly going to continue until this question was answered. Once asked, the question wasn't going to go away. What was normal?

And where could Mary bring this question? To the men in her life? To her husband and her father who, while well meaning, were telling her it was time to move on? To her mother who grieved so with her, that to talk about the baby at all was to invite more suffering? To friends she saw infrequently? How fortunate, how truly heaven sent, was the friend who knew before she saw. "Did you have a bad day?" How fortunate to have someone who had shared all the delight of the pregnancy to remember not only the pain, but the joy as well. How fortunate to have someone connected.

It wasn't a miraculous thing, this sensing, this feeling Julie had experienced that told her Mary was having a bad day while on vacation. No one made it into something it was not. But it was a sensitivity. One young mother realizing that another might, on this "getting away" vacation, mourn once again the child who had died. It was a sensitivity perhaps based on the shared pregnancies or the reality of Julie's own five-month-old. It was a sensitivity of time and space, of the good worker in Julie seeing beyond the work that needed to get done and extending the time of sensitivity to the wounded among us. And to extending that sensitivity beyond work as well. To bringing it home with her, where, on a day in February, she gave it room to bring Mary something more.

I V

HOPE

On that cold February day, Julie was home trying
to take a rare nap. Yet she was thinking about
Mary, her mind wrestling with the pain Mary
had faced, tossing to and fro, as one does before sleep,
with the sadness of the tragedy Mary had suffered. The
conclusion of this fitful reverie was that she heard a Voice
say, "God Bless Mary."

Julie told me she began to sob when she heard the
Voice. I knew right away that she wasn't talking about a

biblical pronouncement from on high. She wasn't having a Moses type of experience when she heard the Voice. She was reaping the benefits of having turned within. She was hearing the quiet Voice of wisdom. She was letting a knowing Voice rise out of her subconscious and speak to her. And she brought the message of that Voice to Mary.

And Mary, who had taken what had happened to her daughter and tortured herself with it, making herself "bad" because of imagined things she might not have done right, imagined things she could have done to prevent the unpreventable, took the words "God Bless Mary" and hung on to them. They were a gift, a prized possession. All she had to hang on to. All she had to tell her, "Maybe God wasn't punishing you, after all."

Mary took the words and believed in them. She didn't question from where they came. She didn't ask by what right or power Julie brought them to her. She *received* them. From her turning within she had learned how to receive.

I often wondered, after that, how quickly things would have moved forward had Julie had more time to herself. We are talking about a woman with two young children. A woman who worked full time. A woman whose husband worked long hours in his own business. A woman who still tried to do it all and do it all well. Because it seemed as if every time this small and seemingly delicate woman found time to be alone, she experienced another connection to Mary. It became apparent that this woman whose life was so full that she barely had time to think of her own needs had somehow made herself accessible, even in her sleep, to the connection with her friend.

Later in the month, her husband out of town at a conference, Julie was home in bed alone, this time in a sound sleep. She was lying face up, an unusual sleeping position for her, when she felt a hand moving from the right top of her abdomen to the lower left, as if someone were underneath her. It was so real to her that it woke her up. It was like a hand caressing her abdomen.

When she talked about the sensation at work the next morning, Mary couldn't believe it. She was so stunned that she took Julie away from the office and down the hall to the women's room.

She said, "I had the same thing."

It was such an unusual experience. They compared the movement. It was exactly the same. "Right over the womb," Julie said. When she said this, Mary told her, "That's exactly what I thought. Over the womb." What had frightened Julie, alone in her house, her husband out of town, had comforted Mary. Because Mary saw it as a sign of connection to someone else: a connection to Grace.

But as Mary freely admitted, she was at that time crediting Grace with any unusual occurrence. Since December, she had been having the sensation of something hopping on her bed as she was drifting off to sleep. She was comforted by the thought that it might be Grace's spirit. She also experienced the sensation of being tucked in. She felt as if someone tucked her comforter around her sides as she was trying to fall asleep at night.

Being awakened by a hand running across the lower part of her abdomen followed these events. She thought it was unusual but she thought it was Grace. She didn't say anything about it, however. Her musings about Grace visiting from the spirit world were personal, private. She thought, perhaps, that they were the sensations of her grief, that pool she could not pull herself out of. Now she wondered. Had the bond she and Julie shared during their pregnancies somehow transcended the pregnancies, transcended the death of her daughter, her Grace? Could it be that what she felt was more than grief? Was there some connection, some bond, between her and Grace, as there seemed to be between her and Julie? Just the possibility gave her hope. And hope is an extraordinary thing, a healing thing. Mary turned within, and through her connection to Julie, a connection that seemed to come more from within than without, she found hope.

It was all about hope, really—this quest for something more, something beyond the ordinary, something larger than ourselves. Mary, Julie, and I were each searching for this "something more," even though we may have hoped for different results from its discovery. While Mary hoped for relief from pain and for some reassurance that her daughter had passed from this life to something better,

Julie and I simply sought the reassurance that fulfillment could be found within our ordinary lives.

We hoped to see and to connect to some larger purpose. To make sense of our ordinary lives. To make sense of the directions our lives had taken. Why had this tragedy happened to Mary? If the tragedy could be made to fit some larger picture, some higher goal, it might become something Mary could live with and that we all could learn from. This became the beauty of the *spirit sisters,* as we eventually began to call ourselves. As the spiritual quest and the connections continued, it seemed possible that they were connected to what had seemed like the senseless death of Mary's daughter, her Grace. That perhaps Grace had come to lead us all on this journey.

How *holy* the journey became once this thought occurred to us. How important! How hopeful! We did not know. We were only ordinary women going about the living of our lives. But if, *if,* we could somehow give a purpose to something we saw as so senseless and sad, *if* we could be changed, improved, made better by this tragedy, then wasn't that a comfort in itself? Wasn't that a reason to hope?

Mary had been writing to her daughter almost from the moment she knew she had conceived. She kept a journal of her pregnancy and of Grace's life. After Grace's death, Mary began to write on her computer instead of in the journal. One night, after writing to Grace on the computer, she realized the computer screen was still glowing after she had turned it off. She spoke of it at work, sharing another thing with her friend, Julie. Julie, once again, did not let her down. She did not say, "Computers don't glow in the dark." She simply went home, observed her own computer, and reported back: "My computer screen does not glow in the dark."

On February 22, Mary wrote this letter to her daughter:

> I feel as if you have left me somehow. I don't know why. It is as if you have crossed to the other side. That makes me sad. Have you? I look at the computer screen and it is dark, not glowing like it used to be. Remember? Were you trying to communicate with me and I was not ready for it? Well, I am now. I love you, darling, and I cry for you. Don't you see my tears? Don't you know what is in my heart, or do you just see my actions and what is not in my heart? Don't leave me, sweetheart. Are you fading into a place I do not know? Or will you reveal yourself to me? Let me know.
>
> I am your mother, always.

If hope was a healer, so was writing. If there was anywhere Mary could be more open about her feelings than she could with Julie, it was in front of the computer screen. She could write with tears streaming down her face. She could write in the middle of the night when she couldn't sleep. She could write about the problems that came and went between her and her husband. About the joys and pains of the mothering still available to her—the stepmothering. She could disclose her deepest fears, her deepest regrets. She could let sorrow overcome her there as she couldn't at work or even during the daily life of her family.

But soon after Mary had noticed the computer screen glowing in the dark, soon after she had asked her daughter, her Grace, to reveal herself, the computer did reveal something! She had just finished a page of particularly intense writing when the cursor started moving backwards, scrolling up, reviewing all that she had written. When the cursor stopped, it was at a sentence she had written to Grace: "The computer has been our only way of communicating." The screen then gave off a silvery light and the letters turned to sparklers before her eyes. The computer, and Grace, were acknowledging that the communication was real!

And Mary did not have to worry that she had no one to share this amazing occurrence with. She did not have to feel as if she were losing her mind, because she knew there was someone who understood connections. That someone was Julie. And Julie was once again accepting, believing. Why couldn't Grace be reaching out to Mary?

The computer was never the same again. It began to malfunction. It was as if a great energy surge had passed through it and scrambled its circuits. Mary could access only certain files and she began to have a difficult time using the computer for typing. It had been a source of comfort to her and now it was a frustration. What was wrong with it? Should she take it in for repair?

One file that Mary could access contained a note she had written to me. A few months earlier, I had asked her to read my first novel and offer any comments. She had typed her observations and saved them in her computer. One evening, when it was the only file the computer seemed willing to let her enter, she opened it in frustration and watched in alarm as the cursor began to move of its own volition. The note listed two typos she had found in my manuscript along with the page numbers they were on. One of the typos was *christmas,* which I had not capitalized. The cursor simply found the word *Christmas* and would not stray from it. At the bottom of the note Mary had written the words, "Thank you for letting me into your writing world." On another evening, the cursor moved until it reached them: "Thank you for letting me into your writing world."

In another file, another day, the highlighted words, from a message Mary had written to her daughter, were, "Love you, Mama."

And so it began.

V

DREAMS, SYMBOLS, AND PRAYERS

J ulie entered Mary's cubicle one morning and announced, "I think I had an out-of-body experience." Mary said, "Julie, I think I had one four days ago." Mary had been afraid to mention it until it happened to Julie.

Julie's experience:

> Before I went to sleep, I started thinking about Grace, wishing I had seen her, gone to the hospital, been at the funeral. Really wishing I could

see her, feel her. As I was going into sleep—I was still conscious—I started to float above my body about two or three feet. I started to get afraid and suddenly was in a dream.

It seemed as if I was in a hospital room with windows on one end. Everything was white. Mary was sitting on the bed. There was a female presence between us. I felt the presence. I went up to Mary, put my arm around her, put my right hand on her chest, over her heart, and started to say all these endearments: "I just want to run outside and tell everyone how wonderful you are, how much I care about you, how much you mean to me," and on and on.

Then we walked to the other side of the room and in my hands appeared several pictures, ten-by-fourteen-inch pictures, and Mary said she had drawn them. They were incredibly detailed pictures of doves. In the background of each was brilliant yellow, royal blue, white—brilliant, pure color. I kept thinking that I could never duplicate them. I kept flipping through them. All doves. All these beautiful pictures. And then this little voice said, "It's time to go back now." I was back in my body. There was a whoosh of sound. I woke up.

By this time, Mary was crying.

In Mary's out-of-body experience, she had risen above her bed by about three feet and then went back into her body with a whoosh after getting scared. They compared the sounds. Both were exactly the same. It seemed significant that the two events had happened within days of each other. Even more startling was that Mary had a dream in which someone touched her heart:

> I had had a baby and I was calling the hospital to see how the baby was. For some reason, the hospital would not let me take this child home. They had to check on things first. I spoke to a nurse who was somewhat curt with me. I asked her how my baby was and she said the baby was "blind and confused." I thought to myself, "How can I deal with this again? I don't know if I am strong enough. Why can't I have a healthy child? A perfect child like everyone else had?" But that was not what had happened. I knew that the nurse was waiting for some type of answer, that she was hanging on the phone. It was then that I felt a finger by my heart, either in my dream or otherwise. And I knew then that I had to remember to love, that love would be the answer.

Julie showed Mary how she had placed her arms around

her in the dream. It was just how it had felt to Mary in her dream. Someone touching her heart.

Not long after Julie's dream with the dove pictures, a dove swooped in front of Mary's windshield when she was on her way to work. No bird had ever flown so close to her, especially not on the freeway. All of a sudden it was just there. Mary said the dove just "swooped, boom," in front of her. As she was peering over the steering wheel and the dove was flying away, its head cocked and its wings bent at an unusual angle.

Mary was telling Julie about the dove one morning when I came in. Mary asked me if I knew anything about the symbolism of doves. As it happened, I knew that I had just read something significant but couldn't remember exactly what it was. The next day I brought in the passage from Joseph Campbell and Bill Moyers's *The Power of Myth.*

> Campbell: Well, the dove, the bird in flight, is a pretty nearly universal symbol of the spirit, as in Christianity, of the Holy Ghost—
>
> Moyers: —associated with the sacred mother?
>
> Campbell: With the mother as conceiving of the spirit, yes.[1]

First Julie had dreamt about the doves that Mary had drawn, then Mary had the dove swoop in front of her car, and then Mary asked me what it might mean and I brought in the information. It began a pattern. From that point on, I was the researcher.

Some connections just continued to reveal themselves with little effort. Mary's husband, John, purchased a T-shirt at a sale associated with Minnesota Public Radio. The T-shirt had a phoenix on it and Mary recognized, in the shape of the phoenix, the same configuration that the dove had been in when it flew away from her car. Then, the same night, she read an article in the paper about a new restaurant that my husband, Donny, had worked on. It was named The Phoenix because on July 22 (the date of Grace's birth) the building had blown up in a gas explosion. The article was about how the owners had rebuilt the restaurant from the ashes. Mary knew that her attention had been drawn to the phoenix for a reason. She found a book on mythology and read that, according to Egyptian myth, the phoenix was a beautiful lone bird that lived for five or six hundred years and then set itself on fire, rising renewed from the ashes to start another long life. It was a symbol of immortality.

At the very same public radio sale, I bought Mary a

necklace with the figure of a woman sitting in a lotus position. In her lap was a purple stone. I bought it for Mary because it reminded me of a pregnant woman—of the eternal mother. Mary found that the figure on the necklace was the exact same figure that was on the cover of the book she was reading.

Then the second dream came.

Mary came to work one day and said, "I've got this dream to talk about at lunch." Julie told her she had a dream to talk about too.

Mary was already eating at the round conference table we used for meetings and lunches while Julie was writing out a check. Julie was going to finish that and then get out her lunch. Later she would say, "All I remember hearing was Mary saying she had a dream about an African American man and that in the second half of the dream he was in a wheelchair. As soon as I heard that, I couldn't write; I couldn't finish my check. I kept thinking, 'Oh my God, oh my God.' I couldn't sit still. I think I began to pace. The whole rest of the day, Mary and I couldn't stop talking about it. To the last detail, the two men had been alike. We kept asking each other about it, 'Was he old? Was he young? What had it felt like?'"

Both dreams had started with the man standing up—

walking. In both dreams he communicated telepathically. Both women had felt the same unconditional love from him. It seemed as if he had the same mannerisms. Neither Mary nor Julie had talked about their dreams before that day. They hadn't told anyone. They couldn't get over it. I can still recall Julie visibly shaking as they made their comparisons, wondered at the significance. I could understand that it was unusual and significant to share a dream figure. But for the two of them, it went beyond understanding, beyond something they could intellectualize. It was that bond again.

In Julie's dream, the older African American man helped her when she had to stop her car because a gang of young boys was crossing the street in front of her. As soon as the man extended his hand and said, "Don't be afraid. Give me your hand and I'll show you the way," all fear ceased to be for her. She trusted him completely. Every thought that entered her mind, every "if," every "should," was immediately countered telepathically by this man. He did not speak but nodded as he sent thoughts her way, his lips curling a little as he communicated.

In the next scene, they were in the conference room of a nursing home. They were holding hands and the man was communicating messages like, "I want you to come with me." Julie kept thinking, "But I'm married." Then she looked down and saw he was in a wheelchair. She was surprised. He had not been in the wheelchair earlier. But he just kept nodding and holding her hand, as if it didn't matter. As if nothing mattered but the love he was sending her way. He absorbed every thought that was negative and communicated only comforting thoughts to her.

"The feelings of faith, trust, love, and peace of mind I had from that man in my dream have never been repeated." Julie said. "But the words seemed most important: 'Don't be afraid. I will show you the way.'"

In Mary's dream the scene was totally different but the man was the same. Again, he was older, slender in build, and continuously smiled. He communicated telepathically and nodded as he did so. He wore an expression that was always pleasant. In both Julie's and Mary's dreams ". . . the thoughts and the feeling communicated by this man were of constant love."

In Mary's dream she, too, knew that the man wanted her to be with him. She, too, knew that she was married and, although she wanted to give her whole heart to the man, she feared that she couldn't because of her marriage. But in Mary's dream the man had a baby girl who was motherless and Mary nursed the baby. This made the man very happy. He told people, "Look at what she did for my daughter!"

In the next scene, Mary realized that the man was in a wheelchair. He hadn't been earlier. She worried about the responsibility of loving such a man but realized then that she had fallen in love with him. She wanted to tell him, "Don't you know that I am married to someone else? Don't you know that this is asking a lot of me? Why are you so sure this will work?" But she couldn't, because he kept looking at her with such love and gentleness, so much gentleness.

Both Julie and Mary had been most impressed by the love they felt coming from this man, and the understanding. It was as if he was saying, "Others don't understand but I do. I'm old and wise and I know." And he did. Months later Julie was still commenting on the dream. "I never felt so safe in my life," she would say.

Yet they wondered, What did it mean to share a dream figure? To have dream symbolism and the symbolism of ordinary life collide as they had with the dove? To have someone touch your heart in a dream and to find out that that person dreamt of touching your heart?

They realized that the dreams were, quite simply, experiences that were beyond their control, just as Mary's experiences with her computer had been beyond her control—just as their out-of-body experiences had been beyond their control. And experiences that are beyond our control relate to the very core of the way we look at ourselves and our lives.

We may not actually *be* in control, but we spend most of our lives *believing* that we are. So when something happens to us, either externally—such as Grace's death or the near miscarriage of my daughter—or internally—such as in profound dreams or visions—they become transformative events. They transform the way we live.

Mary and Julie's sharing of uncontrollable events seemed no less miraculous to us than their becoming pregnant within days of one another. We did not need to calculate the statistical probability of such events occurring to know they were unlikely. We did not need to add up all the events that had occurred since those shared pregnancies—from Julie knowing Mary was having a bad day, to her hearing "God Bless Mary," to them sharing out-of-body experiences or a dream figure—to know something unusual was happening. It was as if a neon sign was flashing: You are connected. You are connected.

But why? Why was this happening? What was its purpose?

The simplest answer we could come up with was that the uncontrollable events were occurring to do just exactly what uncontrollable events do: to transform their lives.

It was at about this time that I began to envy the connections Mary and Julie were experiencing. Because accepting that Julie and Mary were connected and accepting that a connection remained between Grace and Mary demanded that I attribute these connections to someone or something. And the only source I could attribute these uncontrollable connections to was God. God was becoming visible in my friends' lives. Where was God in my life?

I, like Mary, had begun to use my computer to advance my spiritual life. But nothing exciting had happened. I had started a file, labeled it simply, Prayer, and was using it as a place to draw connections between a spirituality of soul, such as I had been reading about, a spirituality of connectedness, such as that which I was witnessing with Julie and Mary, and religion, which had been with me all my life. The envy I felt over the visible experiences Mary had on her computer and the connectedness that Mary and Julie shared came and went as I searched for my own path and my own way to connect. In the last days of March, I made this journal entry in my Prayer file—an entry which illustrates the feelings I experienced during this period:

> I am stupidly envious of my friend Mary's spiritual experiences which have grown out of great sadness and pain. There is no great sadness and pain in my life right now—not even any great conflict. There is busyness, ambition, creativity, but nothing exceptionally good or bad. And in some ways, it is difficult. It is so new, perhaps.
>
> It is difficult on some psychological level not to be in the midst of something that is so personally moving. I, too, have turned to spirituality in my quest to fill the role that pain and strife so often filled. I am not fool enough to want pain and strife back in my life. And my life is very full, but all in a normal sort of way.

So, the spiritual journey. I don't mean to portray it as second best, as "I don't have anything else going on in my life, so I am going on this spiritual journey." It has called me. It has captured my mind and my imagination. It has led the direction of my thoughts and my writing. And I guess I can only envy Mary if I don't see this as miracle enough for me. I have been envious because her journey is filled with a different kind of miracle.

Mary, Julie, and I were all realizing that God had a hand in the events that were taking place and we all began to try to open the lines of communication by, in one way or another, talking to God. And once we accepted that we *could* talk to God, we opened ourselves to the possibility of being answered. As my Prayer file often answered me. My writing on March 29 concluded thus:

I guess I had to write this to learn that this is the journey appropriate to me. A journey in words. A journey of reading and writing and slow revelations.

We were clearly traveling different roads, each in a way appropriate to us, to what we were going through, to what we hoped to find. But our travels continued to intersect. While the way in which Mary and Julie intersected continued to be more visible and dramatic, the way they intersected with me continued to be more in tune with what was appropriate to me: slow revelations, often received only after I had taken the events I had witnessed or shared and let them have their way with me as I wrote about them. As their journeys were illuminated by the symbolism of dreams, mine was a journey that, from the very beginning, was illuminated by the symbolism of words.

VI

ILLUMINATION

I write fiction and prior to 1994 I read mostly fiction. But around the time of Grace's birth I became intrigued by the books that were showing up on *The New York Times* best-seller list, titles such as *Care of the Soul* and *The Celestine Prophecy* and *Crossing the Threshold of Hope*. I wondered what was going on in the world that people were suddenly reading books by an ex-monk and the Pope. My curiosity led me to purchase and read *Care of the Soul,* by Thomas Moore. I took it to a friend's cabin with me and did something I never do. I used a highlighter. I, the cherisher of books, guardian of bindings, collector of signed first editions, used this book like a manual, a text, a guide. Every page, every paragraph, seemed to speak to me, to soothe me. Soon after the experience, another startling thing happened. I could not go back to reading fiction. I would buy one novel and then another, by authors who had always appealed to me before. But they no longer held my interest.

Instead, *Care of the Soul* led me, over the next year, to other writers such as Joseph Campbell and James Hillman and Carl Jung who discussed various aspects of psychology and spirituality. And the surprising thing was that each book I read validated the experiences that were taking place in my life and in those of my spirit sisters. Each of these respected thinkers accepted a place in life for the extraordinary. Each saw the importance of symbols, of dreams, of examining the unexamined life. They did not debunk anything that was happening, but rather validated everything! Because of my belief in words, my belief in the intellect, beliefs still older and stronger than my belief in spirituality, the final barriers preventing me from fully believing in the extraordinary came down just a bit further with each book I read.

I purchased a copy of *Care of the Soul* for Mary when Grace was in the hospital. Perhaps I bought it because I did not know how to soothe Mary myself. She was being strong. After the first few weeks, she would come into work and stay most of the day, visiting Grace before, after, or on a lunch break, or all three. Having already used a lot of sick leave and vacation time at the end of her pregnancy and in the early days of Grace's life, Mary had wanted to save what she had left. For she had no way of knowing how long Grace would be in the hospital or even that she wouldn't be bringing home a baby who would need round-the-clock care. She wanted to have time available when Grace might need her most and so was willing to sacrifice her present needs for her daughter's future.

Had Mary spent all of her time at the hospital, few of her friends would have seen her. Only family were allowed to visit Grace in the intensive-care unit. The rest of us waited for improvement, hoping a time would come when the visitor restrictions would be lifted. Eventually it became apparent that this wasn't going to happen. So we did what we could, offering books, or meals, or prayers, or all three.

There were days, of course, when Mary would break down, would need comfort, would be comforted. But most of the time she seemed to prefer to lose herself in work. To come to work to be away from the trauma of the hospital for a little while. It was difficult to know how much solicitousness to show, how much to ask. Julie was on maternity leave. Our busy season was over. People were on vacation. It was quiet in the office. Mary came and went. I tried to take my cue for how to act from Mary herself, hoping I could tell what she needed or didn't need from me on any particular day. The weeks went quickly—for me.

Then it was over; Grace was dead. Most of us from the office attended the memorial service along with Mary's family and other friends. A few days afterward Mary was back with us. Julie also returned. Work took on its natural rhythm, with one exception: We talked more. There was an openness about the office. One of our own was wounded. Whatever unspoken rules there were, they were suspended. It was as if by silent yet mutual agreement we had decided that whatever Mary needed was all right with us.

I had been diagnosed, about this time, with fibromyalgia—a malady considered to be a sleeping disorder that affects the muscles—and was finding it hard to get up in the morning. I was often the last one in to work and, upon my arrival, I would often find Mary and Julie huddled together, in one cubicle or another, talking, something that in the days before Grace would have been unusual.

In October, only two months after Grace's death, Mary accompanied me on a business trip to Boston. It would not be the usual business trip any more than the workdays were now usual. We spent a small amount of our spare time sightseeing, but we spent far more time talking. She was reading a new kind of book too. I didn't know what to call them, exactly: psychology, spirituality, personal growth, New Age. We spent a lot of time talking about our various readings. We spent a lot of time talking about Grace. Somehow Grace made the concepts more than concepts. Grace had opened us to hear the messages of the readings in a new way. To make the concepts more relevant to our lives.

Mary and I had grown very close in our own way, an intellectual way, a way that was not untouched by the personal or the emotional. But despite the laughter and tears we shared, and despite our meaningful conversations, I still did not feel the kind of bond the shared pregnancies had brought about for Mary and Julie.

And so, in a very concrete way, it had taken my reading, and my ability to contribute to both Mary and Julie through my reading, to allow me to see myself as a participant rather than as an observer. And it had taken that reading, writing, and observing time for me to realize that I had always had my own role and connection to events even if I hadn't always shared the *miraculous* connections. My observer role was important, as was my presence at work, the discussions Mary and I shared about books, the talks we had about Grace. We all have our own role and each is important. Our connections don't have to be miraculous to be connections.

We *all are connected.* It is only our own inability to *see* our connections that keeps us from experiencing those connections. Whatever it is that keeps us from seeing, be it fear or guilt or lack of desire, is what constitutes the barriers we must overcome.

My reading, but particularly my sharing of that reading, opened my mind enough to see the simple truth of the connections that had been there all along, and as soon as this realization occurred, I began to experience those connections in a new way. I began to dream, and by the end of the month, I had made my first appearance in Mary's dreams as well:

> Julie, Margaret, and I were in a foreign country. Different time. Different place. We had long hair and shawls on our shoulders. We were speaking fluent French.

> Julie, Margaret, and I were in a boat in a cool, shady area with lush foliage. It was beautiful. Julie was in her own world looking at the essence of things—molecules and such. Margaret and I were talking, trying to describe this place. Our feeling was one of serenity. Margaret trailed her fingers in the water. I knew then that these were the Holy Waters.

And finally, Mary and I shared a dream experience.

> Mary: I tried to get into the light. It was coming up from my feet. It was brilliant. Someone was coaching me. I kept trying—so hard—to go into the light but I couldn't.
>
> Margaret: There was a light beneath my feet: a flat bright light with jagged edges, resembling a cartoon depiction of light. I was descending into it.

Now that I was realizing my connections, I could look up information on symbols from my own shared dream image. One of the many definitions of *light*, for instance, was "spiritual illumination." And this was what we sought!

For Mary and Julie the connections began with the shared pregnancies. For me the turning point was the shared reading, the shared learning. Mary asking a simple question, "Did I know . . . ?" "Had I read about . . . ?"

These were the particulars of our different beginnings. And because we were ordinary women, it had taken both the ordinary and the extraordinary to launch them. The ordinary, as with me, was the following of a trend: the best-seller list. The extraordinary were the births, the death.

But as with everything ordinary and everything extraordinary, each contained parts of the other.

In the ordinariness of the trend was the extraordinary:

ordinary people were turning to something besides Prozac to heal maladies ranging from fibromyalgia to sickness of the soul. No huge external events, no world-wide crisis, seemed to launch this trend. It was as if it came leaping out of ordinary life, talking about ordinary life, reaching out to ordinary people. Saying, as it did to me, "It is okay to bring spirituality into your life. It is what ordinary people like you are doing. It is okay."

And from the extraordinary: ordinary. What is more simple, really, than two friends comforting each other? Or more extraordinary than that comfort extending into the world of dreams?

How could there be a phrase simpler than "God Bless Mary"? Yet how extraordinary that it came as a gift from one friend to another.

How natural that a grieving mother would write to her daughter. How miraculous that her daughter would respond.

How natural that we came to see our connections to one another before we could come to see the miraculous force that was behind those connections.

VII

RELIGION AND SPIRITUALITY

K nowing that our connectedness came from a
source greater than ourselves caused us each to
look at religion in a new way.

Having found that the Lutheran religion of her youth
didn't speak to her, Julie attended several churches in her
community hoping one would attract her, or at least not
discourage her with talk of sin and judgment. Mary,
although confirmed in the Presbyterian faith, was, of all
of us, the one who had made the most conscious choice

to exclude "organized" religion from her life. Yet she, too, sought something now from formal religious practice. Neither found what she was looking for.

In fact, after searching for a religion in which to belong, they were unsure whether they *wanted* to be religious. They felt more of a distinction than I did between spirituality and religion. But there were no meaningful distinctions between us when we talked about God. And we were beginning to talk about God.

We had never talked about God before. And this wasn't peculiar to our relationships with each other. God just hadn't been a subject that came up in our lives or our conversations with anyone. We, like most people, had discussions of right and wrong, morals and ethics, that occasionally, at least in my household, touched on the subject of God in an obscure way, but this was different. Now God entered through the door of speculation. Through the journey itself. What was life supposed to be about? What did it all mean? God was suddenly part of a larger context. He was no longer, even to me, about going to church. He had become part of a search for meaning.

Into this ripe field of readiness, Julie had brought Mary the message "God Bless Mary" and began to turn her thinking about God from punishment to redemption. Into this field of readiness, our reading had begun to deliver messages that said crazy things like God wanted us to be happy and that we were entitled to a world of abundance. Messages that said suffering and strife were not the preferred state for God's children. We had met the paradox of God being both a God of love and a God of punishment. Up until now we had heard too many messages about wickedness and punishment and hell.

Now we were hearing the messages of love. Was it because that one message, "God Bless Mary," delivered from one friend to another, had opened an unseen door? A door that allowed us each to find what we were looking for no matter how different the ways in which we looked were?

As my reading and talks with Mary and Julie seemed, in one sense, to be leading me away from religion as I had always known it—the religion of my youth, the religion of the parents and grandparents with whom I had prayed the Rosary and listened to Bishop Sheen, the religion of my small parish church—in another sense, they brought me back to it.

I attended a Maronite Catholic church, the parish of my Lebanese husband's family and the Lebanese community that still flourished in my area of St. Paul. It was a rather old-fashioned church and this was part of its charm. I adopted the parish when I married because of its strong sense of community. When I was in fifth grade, I was switched from a small, close-knit parish and small parochial school to a large one that seemed impersonal in contrast. My mother said I almost had a nervous breakdown when this change occurred. My husband's church was like returning to that church and school of my youth, the parish where I had so felt that I "belonged."

But while I loved how all the members of my husband's church knew one another and treated one another as family, I had felt a bit like an outsider. While I loved this parish's ethnicity, seeing it as honoring my husband's culture, I had felt I could never really be a part of the Lebanese culture so evident there. And while I loved this church's traditional atmosphere, the richness of its rituals, the prayers said in Aramaic (so reminiscent of the Latin of my youth), I had not expected to find, in the difficult-to-understand English of its Lebanese priests, priests who seemed of an earlier era, the kind of sermons or discussion of spirituality I was looking for.

But now a change occurred. I began to feel as if I belonged. Because I was beginning to understand what it meant to belong—to be part of something, to feel connected to something. I heard the messages within the Mass differently and I took them to heart. The gospels and sermons no longer seemed to be so full of wickedness and punishment. They were the same gospels, the priest was the same priest, but I was different, and so what I heard was different. The ritual I had always loved was now more than ritual. It had meaning.

As Lent moved slowly toward the holy season of Easter, I knew that I approached a season of rebirth. The externals of my life were the same as the year before almost without exception. I had the same job, the same husband, the same children, but I had not seen the connectedness of them all until I learned connectedness with Mary and Julie. As long as I believed I couldn't be fully accepted in my husband's church, I couldn't be. As long as any of us hold ourselves back from anything, we cannot fully connect with it.

Julie, Mary, and I still held ourselves back from life on many levels, but we each did it in different ways. We were fine people, close to our families and friends. We did good deeds, we did our jobs, we took care—*took care*—of everything but ourselves. But it was in not caring for ourselves that we had suffered the feelings of isolation, deprivation, and unworthiness that had kept us separate. The good people of my church did not *not* accept me, the wife of one of their own, the woman who had become part of their family and their culture when I joined, through marriage, the family of my husband. Yet how could I see this when I hadn't even seen that I had joined my husband when I married him? I had seen the ceremony and the ritual of the marriage but I had not felt it inside. It had not changed me. Because I was still holding back. Holding back all those parts of myself I had deemed unworthy.

It didn't matter that I went to church on Sunday and that Mary and Julie didn't. It didn't matter that Mary was technically Presbyterian and Julie Lutheran and I Catholic. What mattered was our attitudes. When we learned to connect with one another, we had come as close as any of us had ever come to true religion or true spirituality. Our attitudes had become prayerful and God had answered our prayers by giving us each other to learn with. We were beginning to sense that our relationships with each other might just be the chosen method by which God would show us how to connect with Him. Now all that was holding us back were our ideas about ourselves, our pride in our individuality, our continuing belief in our separateness.

VIII
CONNECTIONS

I f there was one thing that Mary, Julie, and I had in
common as a personality trait, it was being individualists. Fierce individualists. We were not dependent
women. All three of us, to the casual observer as well as
to those who knew us well, were seen as capable, hard-
working, independent women.

We did not see being independent, yet, as solitary or separate. We saw being independent as a goal we had achieved.
Something to be clung to and defended at all costs. We saw

independence as the ability to stand on our own two feet, make our own choices, be in control of our own destinies. It didn't matter that we had no idea where our destinies might lead, only that we felt in control of the choices we made as we stood on our own two feet to get there.

Think, for a moment, of all the people of the world standing thus, alone. Think for a moment of one person close to you: a parent, spouse, friend. As close as you are to this person, what really connects you? Often it is a shared past. At other times shared interests. And yet, even with the closest of friends, lovers, family, there is no doubt that you are separate individuals. Being a separate individual is the primary principle of life, begun at the moment of birth when we separate from our mothers. Never again are we anything but separate. Never again are we anything but alone.

While we might spend our lives seeking closeness with others, we know there is a boundary past which that closeness cannot cross. No matter how close we might become, our lives are still our lives. Theirs are theirs.

We shared these beliefs in the individual, guarding and at times flaunting our individualism, our separateness. We did not want anyone to tell us what to do. We did not want to be followers. We did not want even to be too closely identified with any particular group. Our individuality was what we had fought to gain from our parents, fought to retain in our marriages, and cherished as that which separated us from the crowd.

We took pleasure in our distinctive characteristics: Mary had a flair with jewelry and accessories; I presented a classic, tailored (rigid!) look; Julie was proud of procuring the best names in clothing designers at the lowest used-clothing-store prices. Our tiny cubicles had our distinct marks on them: Mary's had a little lamp on the desk for proper lighting, artistic prints on the wall, a framed photo of her husband taken on the day he had proposed, one of her stepdaughter, Amanda, at the piano. Mine had a vase of silk flowers in the window and the most copious display of photographs: my husband and me on our wedding day, my son's formal photograph in his Navy uniform, my girls as first-graders and my girls in high school, my mom and dad, all my siblings, and even nieces and nephews, former employees and students. These photographs hung about, some in frames, others tacked with stickpins to my cubicle walls. Julie, like Mary, had only a select few photographs of her husband and children framed on her window ledge. But she also displayed there a small and cherished gift from her husband, Kelly, a delicate box made of fine basket weaving with a hinged lid that tied closed. We liked these outward symbols of our uniqueness.

Often our greatest vices were held up as badges of our individuality: "That's just the way I am." And there was great opposition to change in this stance of individuality, in the declarative statements of "That's just the way I am." Not because we necessarily thought we were so great, but because we thought we *were* those things we had identified as unique to ourselves, and without them, who would we be? Who would we *be*?

Even when some of those things that marked us as individuals kept us in seemingly eternal cycles of self-sacrifice and strife, we clung to them. When challenged, we only pulled them about ourselves more closely, making of them a cloak and a shield. They were the known of a great unknown world. They were security.

Our idiosyncracies were built upon survival—whatever had gotten us through the many ages of our lives, the many phases, troubles, challenges, successes. If being controlling worked, then controlling was what we would stay with. If "doing it all" had kept the family functioning, then that was what we had to do. If being silent when we wanted to speak out had created less conflict than it had caused, we remained silent.

We were imprisoned by the ordinary and the familiar selves we had become.

So, what happened? What shook up the status quo? What broke the familiar patterns of a lifetime? What created an unusual year?

Birth . . . and death . . . and most important, the realization that what comes in between is not meant to be suffered through alone and lonely. The realization that there were things that connected us to one another, things that kept us from being separate and singular. That no matter how hard we might try to maintain our individualism, we still could not escape the bonds of love. The realization that what was unseen about us and others was just as real as the seen.

Where was the bond between Mary and Grace once the umbilical cord was cut? Between any of us and our parents and our children? Because these bonds are unseen does it mean they are not there? As soon as the unseen was given a little bit of room to express itself, as soon as we began to recognize it, the rest had to follow. Had to.

If I was not my business suit, who was I? If I cut my long hair, would I change any more than Mary did when she changed her hair color? Yet having long hair was, to me, part of who I was. Part of my individuality. Being able to control things and always make them right somehow was part of Mary's identity. Faced with a world she could not control and could not make right, what choices were left? Julie had been used to being able to do it all and do it all well. If a second baby made that impossible, what were her options?

There was not one thing going on but many, just like in any ordinary life. The difference was that we had started to experience connections. Connections that revealed that we were not as alone as we had once thought. Connections that asked us to look at the unseen instead of the seen for answers. So Julie, instead of looking for a babysitter or a housekeeper, instead of looking for externals, turned to look within. So Mary, instead of giving up on a world she could not control, turned within. So I, the silent observer observing them both, began to believe, and in my belief, had said, "Take me there too."

For this turning within was not the turning within of isolation. It was not the kind of self-involved soul searching of the usual, normal, ordinary identity crisis. It was not self-improvement. It was different and at first indefinable. It was a connectedness that went beyond the normal and the ordinary. Connectedness that came from within rather than from without. That came from the real self rather than the surface self. A connectedness that revealed choices we had not known we had. A connectedness that brought us each to the point of wondering: If there is really a choice between being separate and alone or being connected, why can't I opt for the second choice? There seemed to be only one thing stopping us.

IX

JUDGMENT

While we continued to judge ourselves and find ourselves lacking, while we continued to withhold parts of ourselves we didn't deem worthy, we couldn't fully experience our connections. Because we couldn't fully be. The concept of "suspending judgment" related directly to our inability to be our true selves because it related directly to how we thought about ourselves and the world we lived in.

The first day Mary brought the phrase "suspend judgment" into work to share with us, she had us laughing until we cried as she described walking from the parking lot and trying, as she walked, to suspend judgment. Every time she talked about it, she would pantomime the act of suspension. She jerked as she showed us literally what had accompanied her mentally on her walk. Every other step was one in which she had to suspend movement because her mind had issued another judgment. She would walk, halt, walk, halt, all with her own dramatic refinements added. The phrase became a catchphrase that we uttered a dozen times a day. "Suspend judgment."

What Mary had us laughing about was the senseless series of thoughts that ran through her mind in a matter of minutes—the few minutes it had taken her to walk into work. We could laugh because they were the same kinds of thoughts that ran through our own minds:

"I shouldn't have worn this outfit today. It makes me look fat. I wouldn't look so fat if I hadn't been eating so much. Boy am I stupid. I have no self-control. Hey, there's someone even fatter than me. She must really not have any self-discipline. I wonder if anybody else is at work yet. I'm always late. Why can't I get it together? Why does everybody else seem to be more together than me? Of course, I can't help it if no one else in the house does what they're supposed to do. How can I get ready on time when they're not organized? I wish they'd help with the laundry. If I'd had the laundry done everything would have gone smoother this morning. I would have had time to make breakfast. I'm a terrible person for not giving my family breakfast."

Each of these thoughts could produce whole tangents of other thoughts, all of them judgments. The laundry might conjure up all the stains we hadn't removed that our mothers could have, or the idea that if we were really good mothers, we would have used cloth diapers. The expensive wool sweater we had accidentally washed and ruined could lead to worry over the dry cleaning bill that was too high and on to all the bills that were overwhelming and to how much money each member of the family spent. Comparison, resentments, anxiety would grow. These were the things that would produce those attitudes we walked into work with and that would find us feeling relieved to fall into work's rhythm.

Recognizing the way we thought, as with any other realization, was the first step toward being able to do something about it. Just as an alcoholic first has to recognize and admit to being an alcoholic, our recognition of the content of our thoughts led us to admit that we were obsessive judgers.

We really felt we had come a long way toward advancing our spirituality, to being kinder, gentler people, and now this! Had we made any progress at all? But we did not ask this question with hopelessness. We just laughed and saw how much further we had to go. We just laughed because we could laugh—because we weren't alone, because we were no different from one another.

Mary's pantomime of suspending judgment with her body, "My house isn't neat enough"—halt—"I'm late again"—halt—"Everyone else is more together than I am"—halt—besides being funny, was a wonderful learning tool because we realized judgment was not of the body. Judgment was of our minds, of our thoughts. And our thoughts were something we could learn to control!

Like Mary, Julie and I tried. We had no more luck controlling our thoughts than Mary had. We walked haltingly in our suspended state. But we walked with the knowledge that we were not alone. And we walked with new confidence. We had identified a problem that we could actually do something about. We might not be able to do it yet, but we could learn to.

It was a bit like problem solving. Thoughts that made us feel bad had not done us any good, had not served any purpose. Even if at first we could not accept feelings of worthiness, of goodness, we could accept that we had been involved in a thought process that had not worked. It was time to approach the problem from a different angle. It was time to suspend judgment, if we could, and see where it might take us.

Nothing about the spiritual journey was fast. It was not a quick plane ride but a slow ocean voyage. So it was with "suspend judgment." We "got it" right away. We understood it. It was a concept that was supported by our various readings, that took up residence with us and stayed with us throughout the year. Yet we never *achieved* it. It was not an act, like saving a thousand dollars, that had a beginning, middle, and end. It was with us in the beginning of the year and with us at the end and it will stay with us for life.

I tried to tell one of my other friends about what I was learning through my new kind of readings, how excited I was about them and about how they were making me feel better about myself and helping me grow. He said he had gone through a similar phase, but it hadn't lasted.

The thought appalled me. That this might be a phase I would grow out of. I told him so. And he said, "So what if it is a phase? I went through a phase of learning how to cook too. I'm not in that phase anymore but I'll always know how to make croissants."

I shared this conversation with my spirit sisters, as it seemed quite profound. What we learned would be forever! It would be nice to think of reaching a place where we judged no one, not even ourselves, but if we were reminding ourselves at seventy to suspend judgment, we would still be suspending judgment.

Suspending judgment had another side to it, of course: suspending judgment on other people. At first it seemed the far easier task. It was, after all, a more familiar concept. We were raised with the notions of "Judge not your fellow man," "Cast not the first stone," "Walk in her shoes." All those notions from every major religion asked us not to judge others. Just ourselves. And we had learned that lesson well.

If only we had learned to *not* judge others as well as we had learned *to* judge ourselves! It reminded me of a conversation I had with Mary one day about the ego. I viewed the ego as the part of me that said, *You're better than so and so.* It was the part of me I had to only occasionally fight down because most of the time I was thinking, *So and so is better than me.* Mary viewed her ego in exactly the opposite way. What we hadn't realized was that either way, what came from our egos was judgment. This helped us to realize that our judgments were always reflective of how we felt about ourselves!

If Julie felt as if she were somehow lacking as a mother, even though she could not point her finger at anything she was doing wrong, she made her husband see her as lacking. When he walked in the door, she put thoughts in his head—her thoughts! While he was much more likely thinking about a hot shower and a good meal, she had him thinking, *What have you been doing all day? Why should you be tired when all you have had to do is care for this one little baby—a baby you love, a baby you wanted more than anything in the world, the baby you are so lucky to have.*

When my twenty-one-year-old son had problems, I heard everyone blaming me. "If you had been a better mother when he was two, this wouldn't be happening."

Mary actually thought she heard people wondering what she had done wrong to cause her tragedy.

We truly believed people thought this way! Because we had never questioned our own judgment before. Once we suspended our judgment, even for a moment, a step, for one small situation, we began to automatically suspend the judgments we placed on others for us.

We learned this even with each other. When one of us would come in and be having a quiet day, another would invariably wonder, *Are you mad at me?* It took a long time, even among ourselves, even as far as we had come, before we started asking the question. "Are you mad at me?" Asking the question was a suspension in judgment. It was being willing to give the other her own thoughts and release her from ours. And never did the one having a quiet day come back with, "Yes. I am mad at you." It was almost always something totally separate from us.

Mary's discovery of "suspend judgment" was mine and Julie's as well. We would each read, find something that moved us, and bring it in to share. Each of us had a continual feeling of bringing forth ideas of value.

"Suspend judgment" was of great value. We continued to relearn its lesson, under different names, for many months, but its initial lesson was perhaps the most important: There was one thing in the world over which we did have some control—our own thoughts.

While we realized that we could make fairly easy progress in turning off our thoughts about laundry and housekeeping, we also realized concerns about laundry and housekeeping were the result of larger issues that needed to be dealt with. We had to learn what those larger issues were before we could control the thoughts they produced.

It didn't take us long to see that the almost unequivocal answer to where our judgmental thoughts came from was guilt. And that, unfortunately, nothing in our lives was more guilt producing than our mothering and issues concerning mothering.

X

GUILT

Wh19at was so easy to see and define and understand in Mary's case, no matter how unjust,
was that she could not escape going through
a period of guilt, of judging herself, concerning her
daughter's death.

My guilt, for having been a bad mother when I was first
a mother, was hidden, secret, a constant judgment that
had endured twenty years. I had been too young, too
ignorant, too selfish, too lazy. I had not changed diapers
often enough, not been sanitary enough, left my children

too often with baby-sitters. I had slept too late, stayed up too late, not read enough books, not brushed enough teeth, not given enough baths, not prepared enough nutritious meals. I had not provided the best father.

I could look, now, at my daughter's girlfriends and recognize the ones who were like me, whose very presence announced that they were "trouble waiting to happen." Their lives were already set on a path of misery. They were going to fall, not choose. Fall from one thing to the next as if in a dream, accepting no control.

I would see these sensitive girls whose sensitivity was so beyond reach, so wounded, so withdrawn, begging to be touched and screaming *don't touch me,* and I would see myself at their age, so raw, so alone, so wanting. I was one of those girls who thought a baby would fill the void. Who so wanted someone to love me unconditionally that I was willing to produce that someone out of my own flesh and bone. My desire had nothing to do with taking care of another human being. It was just sheer desire, sheer longing.

I carried that desire and longing with me from early adolescence through my mid-twenties, through three children, and through marriage and divorce. I let it incapacitate me. I let it keep me from living a life that made any sense. I continued to fall from one thing to the next until I could fall no further. By my early twenties, I had fallen into the rock-bottom pit and thus was forced to begin my upward climb. I never quite defined where all that longing and all that misery had come from, I just started building a life that worked because I had to.

My girls were still babies, but my son, by this time, was almost seven years old. Where had his childhood gone? And what had I given this child in all that time? How had I damaged him?

Julie's guilt was the most ordinary, the guilt of every new mother trying to do her best and certain her best was not good enough. But added to it was the guilt she felt, again no matter how unjust, of having had a healthy baby when Mary had not, of not having been there for Mary during Mary's tragedy.

For Julie had been a new mother in the weeks of Grace's short life. She had been at home with her new son, unable to visit the hospital, to offer Mary comfort. Unable, because of a prior commitment, to attend the memorial service. Unsure, perhaps, that Mary wanted her, the mother of a healthy newborn.

And what was worse was that she hadn't even felt grateful for those weeks of being home with Peter. Her husband, Kelly, was preparing for the opening of their business, a guest residence for university faculty. They had purchased a run-down fraternity house and, with little assistance from anyone other than his brother, Kelly yet know the extent to which Mary tortured herself with "what ifs?"

Each of us was stuck in the "what ifs?" of the past. How would things be different if we had done things differently? Each of us felt as if we had missed some golden opportunity to do things just right, to do things perfectly. Each of us was certain we hadn't always made the right choices, but that we should have. We knew we had made some mistakes, and that we shouldn't have. We should have been perfect, but we hadn't been.

It wasn't out of our hands, our control. Or was it?

We encountered teachings that tried to tell us that there could be no mistakes because everything happened according to a grand plan. We found these particularly in the Emmanuel books, books that were supposedly messages from an angel told through a woman named Pat Rodegast. Each of us found the messages in these books extremely comforting. One such passage from *Emmanuel's Book III* illustrates this:

> Please remember,
> as you walk through your lives,
> that although your breath of creation
> and intent of perfection
> may become grotesquely distorted,
> everything you have ever done
> has always been, at its inception,
> an act of Love.[2]

that longing and all that misery had come from, I just started building a life that worked because I had to.

My girls were still babies, but my son, by this time, was almost seven years old. Where had his childhood gone? And what had I given this child in all that time? How had I damaged him?

Julie's guilt was the most ordinary, the guilt of every new mother trying to do her best and certain her best was not good enough. But added to it was the guilt she felt, again no matter how unjust, of having had a healthy baby when Mary had not, of not having been there for Mary during Mary's tragedy.

For Julie had been a new mother in the weeks of Grace's short life. She had been at home with her new son, unable to visit the hospital, to offer Mary comfort. Unable, because of a prior commitment, to attend the memorial service. Unsure, perhaps, that Mary wanted her, the mother of a healthy newborn.

And what was worse was that she hadn't even felt grateful for those weeks of being home with Peter. Her husband, Kelly, was preparing for the opening of their business, a guest residence for university faculty. They had purchased a run-down fraternity house and, with little assistance from anyone other than his brother, Kelly was turning it into an elegant, antique-filled sanctuary, a cross between a European pension and an American bed and breakfast. That Peter's birth had coincided with the final stages of remodeling—the business was due to open in September—was something no one could do anything about. Kelly had to put in sixteen-hour days. Often he even spent the night. Julie had never felt so alone. Because she was alone. She could not turn to her good friend, Mary; she could not turn to her husband; and she could not even find the joy in her new baby that she knew Mary would have given anything to feel. The combination of events had left her feeling vulnerable and afraid—and guilty.

Julie's guilt, over Mary alone, weighed heavily on her for a year. Until she could share it and let it go. Until she could learn to suspend judgment.

I read, "Guilt takes up all the room love would fill," and realized that I could not fully love my children when I remained guilty, accused, condemned, judged, because of past actions.

And the most illuminating realization was that the only ones who condemned us, who could condemn us, were ourselves. We were continuing to reevaluate the thought processes we had recognized when we learned the concept of suspending judgment and were now taking the concept one step further. We were recognizing that what we projected outward—thinking God or our children or our parents had judged us and found us lacking—was literally contained within us, just as our thoughts were.

We realized we were doing it to ourselves! Once we understood this, we could then ask, "Did we want to do it anymore? Was there some value in it?" Had feeling guilty for twenty years over my first seven years of parenting done anything to make me a better mother? Had Julie's guilt that she hadn't been there for Mary helped Mary or herself? Could Mary's blaming herself for what was clearly out of her hands improve her life in any way?

And if the answer to all these questions was no, then what purpose did any of it serve, other than to make us feel bad? The thought process finally came full circle. That was what guilt was for. To make us feel bad. To make us bad. As if we did not deserve to feel good. As if we were not worthy to be called good.

But I could see that Mary and Julie were good. Mary and Julie could see that I was good. Mary and I that Julie was good. What we could not see about ourselves we could see about the others.

Ironically, the one who had the hardest road to travel was the one whose guiltlessness was clearest. Julie and I could see how absurd it was for Mary to blame herself for what was beyond her control. But Mary? Even we did not yet know the extent to which Mary tortured herself with "what ifs?"

Each of us was stuck in the "what ifs?" of the past. How would things be different if we had done things differently? Each of us felt as if we had missed some golden opportunity to do things just right, to do things perfectly. Each of us was certain we hadn't always made the right choices, but that we should have. We knew we had made some mistakes, and that we shouldn't have. We should have been perfect, but we hadn't been.

It wasn't out of our hands, our control. Or was it?

We encountered teachings that tried to tell us that there could be no mistakes because everything happened according to a grand plan. We found these particularly in the Emmanuel books, books that were supposedly messages from an angel told through a woman named Pat Rodegast. Each of us found the messages in these books extremely comforting. One such passage from *Emmanuel's Book III* illustrates this:

> Please remember,
> as you walk through your lives,
> that although your breath of creation
> and intent of perfection
> may become grotesquely distorted,
> everything you have ever done
> has always been, at its inception,
> an act of Love.[2]

Although we found such messages comforting, we did not necessarily believe either their source or what they said. We were not about to let ourselves off so easily. Even so, we knew the mistakes of the past *were* out of our hands. We couldn't go back and do things differently. We could only go on. The choice was in how we went on. Did we go on with judgment? Or did we suspend judgment?

I had always viewed the mistakes I made as a young mother as something I could never quit feeling "bad" about because they had produced effects. Undoubtedly, Angela, the baby of the family who had been read to less than her older siblings, was the poorest reader. Surely Ian, the eldest, who had given up a large part of his childhood to fill in as the "man of the house," would never have run away from home as a young adolescent if I hadn't screwed up his childhood.

While the notion that results or outcomes were what produced my guilt remained in me, I could never give it up. I had to see that guilt was only correctable at its source—within myself.

And what better example could I have than Mary. If she viewed guilt as outcome, she would always be guilty—for the rest of her life—for the death of her daughter! What greater insanity could there be than that? But I saw it all around me. In other mothers who had lost children. I saw it in my mother-in-law, who said to Mary one day, "You never get over it."

Would never getting over my guilt be any less insane than Mary never getting over hers?

89

I knew there were differences, of course. I knew that Mary had done nothing to cause her daughter's death and that I *had* done things that caused my children's problems. Yes, there were differences. Differences in my guilt and Julie's guilt and Mary's guilt. But guilt was still guilt. The effects of guilt were still the same. Only by looking past what was different in us to what was the same in us were we ready to learn our next lesson: forgiveness.

XI

FORGIVENESS

In a publication prepared for an F. Scott Fitzgerald celebration, Garrison Keillor wrote about F. Scott's life. In one paragraph he talked about how Fitzgerald had drunk too much and smoked too much and spent too much money and generally made a mess of his life. And yet, that one paragraph made me want to do it all with him. It made me want to do it all with him because Keillor had captured the innocence of a young man trying to bring forth something from within himself that was bigger than himself. Because Keillor had talked about it all with such gentleness.

Julie, Mary, and I shared a relationship punctuated by a similar gentleness. We couldn't make it unnecessary for each other to experience what we had to experience in order to learn the lessons we needed to learn, but we could make it easier. The gentleness with which we were treating each other made us want to be where we were even though it was often painful. No one would want to experience the loss of a child as Mary had. No one would choose to struggle with the issues Julie and I struggled with. Just as no one would choose to share in Fitzgerald's problems with addiction. But our problems, like the problems of the addict, called to us to overcome them.

Someone once observed that the relationship Mary, Julie, and I shared had begun almost as a traditional women's group would, with a tight circle forming around a particular issue or need. This comparison implied, however, that Mary was a one-woman issue or the single woman in need—the victim whom our circle formed around. But this was not the case. Mary was never the victim. Mary was never a broken person who needed fixing. Even during the periods of Mary's most intense grief, there was a mutuality, an awareness that we were all in need of healing. Mary never drained energy from Julie and me as a victim might have done. Instead there always seemed to be an energy flow, an exchange that strengthened and never weakened. The only reason I can think of for this occurring was that we were all in the process of bringing forth something bigger than ourselves, just as F. Scott Fitzgerald was. And just like Keillor did, we looked on the process, the bringing forth, with gentleness.

Not overtly, maybe. I never went into work with the thought in mind of being gentle with Mary, Julie, or myself. But as I look back, *gentleness* is the word that occurs to me. Gentleness was the attitude that permeated our friendship and our journey. Because even from in the midst of the work, and the grief, and the puzzles, and the trying to figure things out, we felt a deep respect for the process we were involved in. We were respectful of each other and the journey we were on.

I could no longer look on Mary as ordinary. I could not help, when looking at Julie, being seized with a feeling of anticipation and excitement for what she was becoming. We knew that we were there to assist each other in the transformation. We knew we were there to assist each other in bringing forth all that we needed to bring forth. We were together to hear the dreams, discuss the books, ponder the thoughts. We were together to accept whatever needed to be accepted on a given day. The three of us together created a gentle place where the lessons could unfold and where forgiveness came naturally, as if invited.

Our forgiveness of one another seemed to lead directly to a need to share confessions—revelations that were expressions of our hidden pain and fears. There came a day, for each of us, when we knew we were together to give confessions or to hear them. And on that day a confession was brought forth from within one of us to the gentle place we had created, and there the confession was accepted with the gentleness, the forgiveness, with which the one giving it had known it would be. We had each known that our confessions would be received with gentleness because we each knew that forgiveness had already occurred.

When had it occurred? Perhaps when we stopped judging ourselves and each other. We weren't done yet, with judgment, but forgiveness may have occurred within any one of those singular moments in which we had suspended judgment. Or it may have occurred in one act of gentleness that was recognized in the moment it was taking place as gentleness. It didn't really matter when it had occurred. Only that it had.

The forgiveness we felt for one another seemed to extend across time. A sort of blanket forgiveness that said, "There is nothing you have done or could ever do that would change the love I feel for you." We said the same things to ourselves but the feeling was different. The way we felt about ourselves was almost the reverse. It was as if there was nothing we could ever do that would change our minds about what horrible people we really were deep down inside. It was as if we believed we had done a really good job of fooling people and we hoped we could keep it up even if we couldn't fool ourselves.

Our confessions were about not wanting to fool any-one anymore. Not each other. And not ourselves.

Our confessions happened as a natural outcome of the process of ridding ourselves of things that caused us to feel bad. Our confessions happened because we had grown so close, come so far together that the secrets that remained between us became burdens. But our confessions happened mainly so that we could forgive our-selves.

I don't know why it is that we can look at almost any-one else and say easily, "It does not matter," and then look at ourselves and say, "It matters very much." Or why we can treat others with gentleness and remain hard on ourselves. But this seems to be the way it is. We feel bad about something we have done, bad if we cover it up, bad if it is revealed. We can even feel bad about the thoughts we have toward someone we believe has done something to hurt us.

It was as if we were made up of extremes. One day hat-ing ourselves and one day loving ourselves and accepting neither. It didn't make any sense to accept either because what we hated wasn't ourselves and what we loved wasn't ourselves. We hated our failures and loved our successes. Hated our mistakes and loved our choices that had turned out right. Hated ourselves on the days we had arguments with our husbands, loved ourselves on the days we got along. Hated ourselves on the days we blew up at our children, loved ourselves on the days we treated them with kindness. And even on our best days, we still had the little secrets we hid away, the things we loved ourselves in spite of. It was as if we were too close to ourselves to ever stand back the way we did with each other and say, "You're okay just the way you are." But we were getting closer.

Our confessions were about hope. Hope that one day we could look at ourselves as we did each other and give ourselves that same blanket forgiveness. Our confessions brought forth those things that might make that forgiveness possible someday. They brought forth that which we most needed to heal. They were brought forth so we could see that it wasn't the confessions themselves that mattered but the forgiveness. So we could see that forgiveness was a prerequisite to bringing out something bigger than ourselves. So we could see that lack of forgiveness would forever keep us small. So we could see that bringing forth anything from within was a liberation. Our confessions happened so that we could see that forgiveness would set us free.

Like our guilt, the mistakes that we needed to confess were different from one another's. But the need to confess was the same. And the need for forgiveness was the same.

And just as our guilt was concentrated around our issues of mothering, our confessions, too, had a common theme. Even though we made small confessions here and there concerning imagined slights or situations we saw as competitive and consequently divisive, our major confessions were about our distant pasts. They were about the things we thought could change the way people felt about us. They were the things we had been too ashamed to speak of. They were like sins of omission. The things we hadn't told.

Forgiveness was looking back not with judgment but with gentleness, as Keillor had looked back on Fitzgerald's life. It was taking the pain out of the looking back—not glorifying it, not oversimplifying it, not condoning it, but also not condemning it. Accepting it as what was.

Both the confessions and the forgiveness were acts of sharing.

Both the confessions and the forgiveness released us from the limits we had placed on ourselves and on our friendship. And with that release we were freed. Free to connect in the way we had each seen we wanted to. Free to share without limits.

XII

SHARING

Without the sharing that was going on each day there would have been no movement, no hope, no connections, no forgiveness.

Think of all the moments in your life that might have been breakthrough moments if you had only had someone to share them with, someone who believed in you and in whatever inspiration had come to you!

That was what we had. Every day, every week. Someone listening. Someone caring. Someone who was also looking at the bigger picture. Someone who believed there was a bigger picture at which to gaze. Someone who we knew would not make us feel foolish. People to whom we could tell, quite literally, anything. We trusted each other long before we trusted ourselves.

Although our story here is the journey of the three, and the events written about have emphasized that journey, there were also three individual journeys going on. Three journeys to the center of the self. And each self was supported by two other selves! That support, that sharing, brought the three journeys together and made them one.

Imagine, if you will, how different Mary's story might have been without the shared experiences. Mary at times called me the "fearless" one, but it was often Julie who led the way. Julie who opened the doors by asking, "Did you have a bad day?" by saying, "God Bless Mary," by admitting, "I think I had an out-of-body experience."

Without the support that came from that act of sharing, what might Mary have done with her grief? Or, perhaps, more accurately, what might grief have done with Mary?

It came to us clearly now—that the bonds, the connections, the sharing were what was important. They, more than the internal life, the turning within, were the essence of it all. As important as our individual discoveries were, the sharing was what taught us the most.

In the schoolroom of three, all the lessons were available to learn, because beyond the teamwork, beyond the friendship, beneath the bonds remained the stuff of humanness, of day-to-day life to sort through. Could we really trust? Really love? Could we learn from each other how to believe in ourselves?

Mary and I were both old enough to be having what society might call an "early midlife crisis." As defined in the dictionary, *midlife crisis* is "the sense of uncertainty or anxiety about one's identity, values, relationships, etc., that some people experience in midlife." Having a midlife crisis would be seen as a fairly ordinary thing for women of forty to be going through.

But we did not call it midlife crisis. We did not call it searching for God, either. If we called it anything, we called it a spiritual quest. And although the stirrings of the quest could be traced in each of us to a time before Grace, it had been Grace who brought them into the present, the *now*, Grace who made the journey *holy*, and Grace who made continuing a necessity for each of us.

For a necessity was what it had become. Not in a dutiful sense, but in the sense of inspired, excited learning. We gathered each day, grateful students in a classroom of our own making. And the more we learned, the more we wanted to know. Our readings now encompassed subjects we had once thought of as disparate and, more than that, totally uninteresting! It was as if someone, could it be Grace? was leading the way for us and we had to follow— *had to.*

Without the act of sharing with Julie and Mary, I would never have read about angels, read the inspiring words of the spirit Emmanuel, would never have gone beyond the intellectual, the safety of the trends in my pursuit, would likely never have created a computer file called Prayer and used it for prayer, would probably never have talked about my spiritual experiences at all—and never have received the benefits of the second kind of sharing: sharing outside of the group.

While I was content to leave my spirituality behind closed doors, both that of my work and home offices, Mary and Julie, to my continual surprise, were willing to speak of what was happening to them within a larger realm. When Mary told me, one day, that she had shared her computer malfunctions both with her mother and mine during an afternoon at her mother's home, I was truly shocked. "You did what?" I asked. "What did my mother say?"

That my mother had listened and seemed to accept Mary's story with her usual grace made me wonder. *Could I talk to my mother too?* But I did not. I assumed my mother's acceptance of Mary's story was the acceptance of politeness, the acceptance of Mary's grief, the acceptance of another woman's daughter. I assumed she would judge my journey, my revelations. I assumed she would find me unworthy of them.

But still, I gloried, hanging on to the stories of every encounter Julie or Mary had in which they reported, "I heard this voice say . . . ," "I felt a hand over my womb . . . ," "Someone touched my heart . . . ," and for their bravery brought back treasures. Simple acceptance. Wonder. Awe. Envy. And information. Someone would suggest, "It reminds me of something I read about . . ." in this book or that . . . and we would have a new source to turn to. Someone would compare a dream to a myth . . . and we would have a new source to turn to. Another would say, "I remember when something similar happened to me . . ." and we would feel still more accepting of our own experiences.

To my surprise, each time Julie or Mary spoke of the Grace miracles, of their feelings of being on a journey, of the signs they were beginning to see to lighten the way, other people shared similar stories and offered new avenues we could explore. Each of these encounters was legitimizing. The part of me that was squeamish about angels and the spirit world was beginning to give way.

When I said, earlier, that I kept my emerging spirituality behind closed doors, I meant it literally. I had been acting as if what I was involved with were some kind of perversion. If my husband walked into the room while I was typing in my Prayer file, I immediately scrolled up so that my computer showed a blank screen. While I would read books on science or psychology openly, I had kept books such as the Emmanuel books concealed, hidden under my side of the bed or in a bathroom cupboard. While I talked to Julie and Mary freely and openly about God and every other subject that concerned me, and spoke to a few people about the "intellectual" reading I was doing, I had talked about what was happening to us to no one else. Not one person.

Part of the reason was that despite my religious upbringing and beliefs, all the images I had in my mind of overly religious people were unappealing. I did not want to be a religious zealot. I had other plans for my life. I wanted to write mystery novels and smoke cigarettes and be an intellectual. I had no desire to lead a "pure" life. But there was no doubt that, as I had written in my Prayer file back in March, I was being called, and whether I always liked it or not, I was answering the call.

The sharing that Mary and Julie were doing, sharing with professors and health care professionals, secretaries and musicians, people of both sexes and from all walks of life was helping me to see that all kinds of ordinary people who were not religious zealots had experiences or were accepting of experiences of the divine. I was beginning to see that I might be able to be a spiritual person and still be "normal."

But this still wasn't the end of my fear. I also feared the spiritual life because, while I had begun to accept that I was worthy enough to have one, being openly spiritual would give others the opportunity to judge my worthiness. Because I thought they would judge against me, I kept it to myself.

It was only when Mary's and Julie's examples showed me that I had no more cause to fear other people's judgments than I had to fear becoming a religious zealot that

I finally uncovered what my real fear was about.

Like a person not wanting to admit he or she needed to see a therapist or doctor, a part of me did not want to admit I had something wrong that needed fixing. A part of me didn't want to admit that if there was something wrong that needed fixing, I couldn't do it myself.

This was the feeling that had me scrolling up my computer screen when my husband entered the room. I feared he would wonder "what was wrong" that I was turning to prayer. Because a part of me recognized something *was* wrong.

Having arrived at a place of nonjudgment with Mary and Julie was not enough. Having achieved the ability to share with Mary and Julie was not enough. And all of Mary's and Julie's faith in me was not enough. They could take me only so far along the path.

There had been a great exchange of books going on. I bought the intellectual books and borrowed from Mary and Julie the books with the embarrassing covers that I hid under my bed or in the cupboard. But on one spring afternoon when I had taken a walk over to the university bookstore, I purchased my first angel book. I bought about five other books as well and when I got back to the office, I displayed the five "other" books boldly and only shyly brought forth the angel book, saying something like I thought it was a "pretty little book."

It was a pretty little book and that was about all it had

going for it. It was called *Ask Your Angels* and was supposed to be a "practical guide to working with the messengers of heaven to empower and enrich your life." I considered it poorly written and corny. It only took one chapter for me to make this judgment. I spent about another half hour flipping through the rest of the book—I had, after all, spent twelve dollars on it—but then I put it aside. I had five other books to choose from. I went on without giving *Ask Your Angels* another thought.

But a seed had been planted. Mary's and Julie's faith in me could take me only so far. My faith in myself could only take me so far. The divine help that I was so afraid to admit I needed was about to be given to me. All I needed to do was "ask my angel."

XIII

FAITH

On May 1, 1995, I sat down at my computer, as I had sat down at my computer on many other days. I pulled up the file I had labeled Prayer, the same file I had written on many other days. And because I had read that it was possible to contact my angel, I decided to try. I did not expect an answer. One might ask, "If you did not expect an answer, why did you ask?" It is a legitimate question, the answer to which is, simply, that I was ready to ask. I wrote:

Dearest Angel,

I think I have felt you with me since my earliest childhood, certainly in my most tormented times when you would tell me I was special and a part of me believed you. Thank you. That voice that said I was special kept me living as much as I could live. Feeling as much as I could feel. There has always been a wonder in me, something that embraced mystery. It is this part of me that is willing to believe I can talk to you. It is this part of me that says it makes sense. Will you talk to me?

The answer came immediately, my fingers responding and typing the words almost before the thoughts had entered my mind. Like Julie's Voice that had delivered the words "God Bless Mary," mine was also an interior voice. I did not hear a voice distinct from my own. But I knew the words were not my own.

Smell the sweetness. You are sweet. Don't try to force it, to will it, just let it come. It is there in the in between, between thought and feeling. Breathe. Feel your heart.

Why does it feel so heavy? As if it will break?

It's trying to open. To let joy in.

Is that my next lesson?

Yes.

Thank you. What shall I call you?

Peace.

Thank you. You are there in the in between?

Yes. Like white. Like space.

Space between the letters and words?

Like space. Like smoke.

Is it okay that I smoke?

Everything you do is okay.

Really?

If you give thanks for it.

Count my blessings?

No. You are blessed. What you do is blessed. No counting. Look in between.

In between the numbers there are no numbers?

Something like that. You're getting it.

Will you help me with my writing?

I am always helping you.

I want to know if my writing will be recognized. I'm sorry it seems so important to me but it is.

Look in between. This time is in between. Time is in between. Don't worry about time.

Will you help me do that?

Of course I will.

Do you mean that in time I will be recognized, but that there is not time? That's hard to understand.

Everything is. Don't worry about time. This is a very important message. Relax. Smell the sweetness.

I never realized how often time comes up. I was just going to ask, Do you mean smell the sweetness of this time?

Forget time. When it is important that you not be disturbed, you won't be.

Thank you. I like your name.

You gave it to me. It has always been my name. Dearest. Remember to rest.

One of the ways I knew this message had not come from me were those first words from Peace: "Smell the sweetness." I was in the middle of preparing to put my house on the market. I sat at a desk in an unfinished basement surrounded by boxes. The walls and floors were cement. Not ten feet away was the cat litter box. Anyone who has ever been in such a basement would know that "smell the sweetness" would not occur to anyone sitting in it. This is a simple, almost silly explanation of how I knew, but it illustrates the point. From nowhere in my own mind would the words "smell the sweetness" have naturally arisen.

I have come to believe that one of the reasons the words

were so accessible to me was that I am a writer. I am used to going to my computer and turning off the thoughts of the everyday in order to create thoughts about characters or places that live only in my imagination. This may seem like perfect evidence that my imagination created my conversations with Peace. On the contrary: my imagination created the space through which Peace's words were able to enter my consciousness.

Yet, I cannot tell you that I did not question the source of the messages. That there were not moments, from the very beginning, when I wondered, questioned, doubted. But I have chosen to have faith, as I chose to have faith on that first day, as I wouldn't have chosen without everything that led up to the moment.

To have faith or to have doubt. It is the same choice I still face every day. It is not a static choice. I have chosen to have faith again and again. And I know I will need to choose again and again, because doubt has been my companion of a lifetime and we are having a hard time saying good-bye to each other. I continue to choose faith simply because I know that of the two choices, faith or doubt, it is faith that I want to carry with me into the rest of my life. Just as when faced with the choice of solitude or connection, I came to see that connection was what I wanted.

I was afraid, terribly afraid, of what people might think of me when they heard I was talking to an angel. My spirit sisters came to my rescue. First by hearing my story, and later by finding their own angels, Trinity and Water.

After having a second conversation with Peace the following day, I was unafraid enough, I had faith enough, to tell the only two people I could tell, the only two people I felt connected with on a spiritual level. I phoned Julie and Mary at the office (I was taking a few days off to do some work on my house before we put it up for sale). Mary and I spent a few minutes catching up and then I told her: "I talked to my angel." I don't remember having to explain it at all. I remember Mary yelling to Julie so that they could both hear the few details I offered at the time. Within moments they decided this was something we could not share over the phone. They were so believing, so trusting, so intent on hearing a firsthand report of the event that they took the morning off the next day to come and hear my story.

I remember the day vividly. I had just finished stripping the old wax from my kitchen floor and cleaning the room thoroughly. It sparkled. It was spring. The sun was shining and I had big windows that let in the light. I went out and picked some wildflowers from across the alley and placed them in a small vase. They looked delicate and appropriate to the early spring day. And there is something about a gathering of women around a kitchen table, coffee cups in saucers, the windows open to the breeze, the sound of quiet conversation, and the mutuality of laughter. I looked forward to it. I appreciated it as it happened. And I remember it. There is something about things coming in threes.

As soon as they arrived, I explained what had happened as clearly as I could. That I had been painting and that when I took a break, I went to my computer and asked for an angelic communication. I asked because I had read in *Ask Your Angels* that it was possible. But I had been asking for months, as Mary and Julie had. I had been praying, in one form or another, daily. I had been seeking answers. I had been seeking comfort. I had been striving to become a better person, to live a better life, to know how to do that. Literally asking was just the next step in that process.

I did not have a printer at that time. I gave an oral report, but in order to show Mary and Julie the words that had come to me from Peace I led them down into my messy basement to show them the words on the computer screen. I sat in the red wooden chair before the white Formica-topped desk that held my old Mac Classic computer. We read the words together. I told them of how I began to cry immediately as the words came to me. Of how emotional I felt. How I had felt comforted and scared and honored all at the same time.

The day became an important one for me, and I don't think it was an accident that it began with a visit from my spirit sisters and with the love and acceptance that visit entailed. It became the day I opened my heart. The following is an excerpt from the file in which this occurred:

May 5, 1995

Julie and Mary just left. Thank you so much, Lord, for

giving me friends to share this experience of Peace with. Peace, I am sure you were there with us as we talked about you. As Julie said at one point, the whole group of you—all of our angels—were probably getting a laugh out of us. I liked that image.

So do I. It was quite accurate. . . .

My friends were so sweet today. Yet I feel slightly removed from them, from everyone. Why is that?

It is because of your closed heart. Your heart has been closed a long time. Your family has been trying to open it. Listen to them. Let them in. They will not hurt you. . . .

I want to open my heart. What must I do to make it so?

Open it. Imagine a door that keeps feelings in and keeps love out. Here is the key. I am handing it to you. [I see, with my eyes closed, a door that looks more like a window, square and paned, with light only at the edges.] You see, the light was just seeping out the cracks before. Now it is brilliant. [It is.] You didn't need to be afraid to open it.

Now what?

Now prop it open. Here is a brick, as heavy as your heart used to be. That's right. You can keep the brick for a while until you learn to keep it open on your own. It's done. There's no going back. I'll be the keeper of the brick. You aren't to worry about it. When you're ready, I'll remove it. Meanwhile your heart is open. Everything happens for a reason. Remember that. Dearest. And remember to rest.

To have faith or to have doubt. My heart was now open or it wasn't. It all depended on what I chose to believe.

If someone had asked me a week before whether my heart was opened or closed, I would have said, "What kind of question is that?" But now I knew, with no doubt whatsoever, that my heart had been closed and had been closed for a long time. I had known something was wrong that I couldn't fix. I just hadn't known what it was.

Closing our hearts is what we do when we can withstand no more, whether it be pain or disappointment or grief or abuse. It is what we do when life gets to be too much for us and the only way to get through it is to put ourselves on automatic pilot and move through our days without feeling.

Opening our hearts again is another story. Once we have survived on automatic pilot long enough, we don't remember that there is anything to open. We don't realize that when we closed that door to pain, we closed the door to joy and love as well. And when our lives start functioning again and we're ready to feel again, we may realize we don't feel with the intensity of our youth, with the intensity of our "pre-closed" heart selves, but we think it's okay. This is the more mature love of an older and wiser person, we might think. This is a good place, a safe place. It's just enough but not too much.

We don't realize we have lost anything until we begin to seek.

Was my angelic communication real? It was real

enough to bring forth from me the realization that there was something lost that I needed to find. It was real enough to bring forth the question, Why do I feel slightly removed? It was real enough to fix what was wrong.

It was real enough to open my heart.

When I read Emmanuel's books, I decided it didn't matter whether I believed the messages were coming from an angel—all that mattered was that I found the messages comforting, that they spoke to me, that they made me feel better. I felt the same way about the messages contained within the Peace writing. It didn't matter how I was receiving messages, only that I was receiving them.

But I did consider Peace an angel. I considered Peace an angel because it was an angel I had requested communication with and it was Peace who responded. And I considered Peace an angel because I had no other idea of where else communication such as this would be coming from. I might not know what my church would think about an ordinary woman conversing with an angel, but angels were supposed to be a part of the beliefs of my church. Guardian angels had a feast day just as saints did. I had been told as a little girl that I had a guardian angel. I had felt, in some of the worst moments of my life, that I would have despaired of any hope if not for a formless belief I had that someone/something was with me—that there was a reason for hope even when I couldn't define what that reason was. So my history, my beliefs, my recent experiences, and my readings had all converged into the moment that I wrote: Dearest Angel.

I look back now and think how simple this communication was. How childlike. How innocent. How it and all the readings I had so responded to were simply telling me that I was okay. That fragile human longing for someone/something to let us know, to let us believe, that for all our humanness, we are still okay the way we are, with all our imperfections. For how else can we start but from the simple premise of okay-ness? One cannot build on a foundation that is seen as inherently flawed. I was being given permission to begin to build—as, eventually, we all were.

The permission was given through a simple act, an act simpler than believing, an act simpler than having faith. It was given through the same act that gave me communication with my angel. It was given through the act of asking.

Once again, it was Julie who opened the gates, who dared to open herself to the possibilities that asking offered. Julie asked me if I would try to contact her angel.

Just as we had quickly become accepting of Grace communicating with Mary through the computer, within a week some of the awe concerning my conversations with

Peace had turned into acceptance too. I had been sharing the Peace messages that I thought might interest my spirit sisters. While Peace and I talked about personal issues most of the time, his answers had what seemed to be a universal significance. They were the kinds of answers anyone could benefit from.

Julie looked at this new source of information with excitement. While Julie and I did consider ourselves spirit sisters, we both recognized that without the connecting force of Mary, we would never have gotten to know one another. Perhaps we were just two closed-hearted people doing the best we could. Perhaps we were just two quiet people, given to shyness when we were alone together. There was no animosity between us, just a quiet acceptance that we needed Mary's more outgoing personality to draw us out and facilitate our communication. Julie's request, then, was the first tentative step in establishing a more one-on-one bond, and I took it as an honor, a responsibility, and a sign of faith.

On the afternoon she asked me to contact her angel, Julie stood outside my cubicle, talking to me about it. Mary flitted back and forth as was her way and Julie asked, "You want Margaret to ask for you too, don't you Mary?" I took Mary's response, a rather vague "whatever" or "I don't know," as a desire to know but a fear of knowing.

I wanted to ask for both my spirit sisters because I wanted to share the wisdom I had found in the writing in a way that would be more meaningful to them. But I was nervous. My nervousness about asking led me to spend a lot of time just writing before I requested this special favor from Peace:

May 10, 1995

Since beginning to talk to my angel I have not talked to myself much here. As I read over the writing I did before talking with Peace, I realize that I still need this talking-to-myself space too. I have to smile here, because, in Peace's theory of oneness, he and I are one. The physical and the divine are one. So, I suppose, I am talking for both of us here, and Peace, I hope you are with me because my doingness tonight is to be a real message-bearer for the first time. Julie has asked me to talk to her angel and the responsibility of that humbles me.

I am glad I shared with Julie and Mary as I have no idea, still, how to share with anyone else. And it is not just about the angel stuff. It's about me. Is it me who puts the restrictions on myself when I am gathered with other friends? Me who says their stuff is more important to talk about? I suppose it is. Restrictions. Another interesting way to think about what I do to myself. Restricting rather than letting go.

I've learned a lot from listening. I've gotten a lot of good strokes for being compassionate—for suffering with others. But not letting others suffer with me—not letting them be compassionate for me—is robbing them of something.

As James Hillman says in his book *Insearch:Psychology and Religion,* we cannot meet all of our own needs. If we could, there would be no human interaction, no "society." But I can meet the needs of another and another can meet some of my needs; and that is the way of the world. And here I have been all my life, trying so hard not to be needy, trying so hard not to let anyone else see my needs—as if it would make me weak. Hillman also says the needs we deny become demands. I wonder—on whom? I feel as if I have been demanding of myself more than of anyone else. I have been hard on myself.

It's funny walking around with an open heart. One of the strangest physical sensations I've had is of feeling smaller, almost as if I am a child masquerading in adult clothing. Perhaps I am a teen again—back in that time period in which I first closed my heart, like an alcoholic whose development is arrested at the point at which she becomes an alcoholic. Lord, I don't want to be a teen again.

I am avoiding talking to you, Peace, because of this responsibility weighing on me, and I am going to quit avoiding it in a minute. But first I want to reflect a little on what sharing has shown me in the past few days.

There has been some uncomfortableness, some pride, some humbleness, but mostly a feeling of bringing forth something of value. I suppose now that this is because of you, Peace, but not as a substitution for being of me, not in a bad way. Peace, you are helping me learn to share by giving me the opportunity to witness the gift that it can be. Perhaps you are a little like the authors Thomas Moore and James Hillman to me, a way of validating my own knowingness that makes it easier for me to talk about. I have no doubt that you are a good thing, but this is a sort of worldly proof of it for me. Thank you for answering my literal request—for literal messages. I suppose that the act of sharing is a literal, literate way for me to gauge the experience by bringing it outside of myself. And maybe this would be a good way to view all my writing—as a gift I bring literally, literately to the world. Another way to help me let go of the fear of it. A way to legitimize myself. I can hear you saying I don't need to do that and that thinking I do is fear talking, and I'm sure it is, but bear with me for a while on this one. I can also hear you saying that anything that makes it easier and better for me is okay. That all I do is okay. Thank you for that. Thank you for being with me.

I feel your presence often—in the heavy beating of my heart, in the voice that says *stay* in the *now,* in the bird that responds to my being in the now with birdsong. And I know for sure that something happened between us today at the little round table in the office after Julie had said I could ask her angel (although she didn't say what I should ask). I know it was you that brought me the word *tenderness* in regard to her. I know it was you because I got tears in my eyes, as I am getting them now, and because Julie got tears in her eyes. You know what Julie needs to know, or her angel does. And if the image we had at my kitchen table the other day was accurate, as you said, and the three of you angels were laughing along with the three of us women, then I imagine you all know about all three of us.

I can only ask humbly, respectfully, Peace, that you who are so wonderfully and thankfully accessible to me, help me to bring a message from Julie's angel to her, about how she can find that same accessibility.

I had some feelings, some images, earlier that I will start things off with and perhaps the two of you can guide me from there. The images, the feelings I got, were that Julie's insight will come more from the inside out than from the outside in. I say this in relation to myself, feeling as if my communication with you, Peace, is coming into me from you and you being outside of me. I know this inside-outside stuff doesn't make as much sense to you as it does to me, but it is the best way I can describe what I felt about Julie. The other feelings, images, were just this: that it, whatever it is, is close to the surface in Julie, and I had a sense of it coming out her pores, almost like sweat. Can you clarify any of these things, either of you? Julie gave me her permission to ask for her. I believe she truly wants to know her angel. I know she has been looking for something for a long time—a meaning, a purpose, guidance. She has moments of physical sensations when she senses she is close to *it,* but she is becoming frustrated—although that is perhaps too strong a word. You, after all, know her better than I. I am just procrastinating because I don't want to get this wrong and I know if I ask in fear rather than in love, I may get it wrong. So I am going to calm myself now, rid myself of that fear, and ask in love that you give me a message that will comfort and guide her.

Peace, I feel you reminding me that nothing that is said here will be wrong. Thank you.

I am there for her. She is already hearing me. She feels me. I regard her with great tenderness. I guard her, more in the way a mother guards a child than with you and Peace. I look out for her with tenderness, great tenderness and great love. She is very special to me. She is the only one for me. There is no other who could take her place. We are meant to be together. We have been together before. I am almost too attached to her if an angel can be too attached. I cannot keep her from learning painful lessons but I would like to. I very much want to make things easier for her.

I keep getting the word *image* in my mind.

There is a great need in her to do the right thing. Ever since she was a little girl. There was such great sadness in her as a little girl. It is why I regard her so tenderly. If she will let herself feel how much I love her, she will be more open to my beingness. I want to help but I cannot help unless she asks. I am happy she asked you. Tell her to ask me and I will be there where she has access to me. I overflow into her with love. Like a cup running over.

You have made me feel such incredibly strong emotions. I can't keep from crying.

That is how she is overflowing with emotions that can't get out. This image you see is solid with holding in, holding on tight, holding on for all she's worth. Clinging to what she has in great fear, so afraid, so alone. It is why you see images of water and pores and sweat coming from her, she is so overflowing with painful things she hangs on to as if they were her lifeline. There is not something she needs to release, she just needs to release. To quit holding herself together so tightly her skin is taut with it. Her very image will change when she releases.

What must she do?

She must want to be. She must let go. Not in the way you need to let go but to let go of the very lifeline she hangs on to. It is a great leap of faith I ask of her. She and I are one; this asking is not in the way you see it—it is not a demand, it must come from within, from our oneness. I cannot ask. She can. Tell her to ask.

Literally?

Literally.

How will she know you are answering her?

She will know the great relief she feels.

Anything else? Will you talk to her?

If she will listen. I have always been with her. Tell her to release what she holds on to so tightly and I will be there.

Julie related to me later that at the very time I was asking for her, a great feeling of relief spread over her. Her breathing became easier, she felt lighter, she felt a sense of release.

I didn't stop with the response from Julie's angel but went on:

While I am feeling so receptive, I must ask for Mary. Dear Mary. She is unsure she should ask, but I think I have her permission. The images I felt of Mary were that she has so much at stake in opening up. It reminded me of how I felt about my mother. I had told a friend once how judgmental I thought my mother was, and my friend had responded that my mother was more judgmental (than my father) because she had more at stake; she had put so much more effort into raising me, had so much invested in me. And that is the way I feel about Mary—that she has so much invested. And I also had a feeling of her doingness—that she needs to do something. Something with the earth. Something grounding. Can you help with these images? Any of you? Can you give me a message for Mary?

Mary is. Mary is in a state like suspended animation, between the depths of despair and the wholeness of joy. She fears she could go either way, so she stays where she is. This is okay. Where she is is where she is. When she has confidence that she can turn her back on despair, she will turn to joy. When she turns to joy, she will recognize me.

Is there a way you can help her or I can help her or she can help herself turn to joy?

She will when she believes she will. She will turn to joy.

124

And how then, will she recognize you?

In the birds of the air and the seeds of the ground and the smile of a child.

Is there some way she must ground herself before she can turn to joy?

There is nothing she must do. Mary is. Mary is finishing up a long, long journey. She can take her time. I am patient. I have been patient a long time, an eternity. But I am waiting for her with love. Tell her I miss her.

The next day I pulled Mary and Julie out to cigarette break with me to share the writing and to try to explain the feelings that had accompanied the messages. I had been unprepared for the onslaught of emotion that asking for Julie produced. I did not know where it had come from and thought, perhaps, that it was coming from her angel. This led me to speculate that her angel might be a female, even though, I said, I had a sense that the angels were androgynous.

I told Mary that her angel, in contrast, had seemed rather stern—more toward me than toward her. As if he were telling me, "Mary is what she is. Don't mess with Mary." After it became apparent that Mary had not really meant for me to ask for her, the source of this sternness seemed justified—as if I were being rebuked: "Don't mess with Mary." I wrote later about my concerns:

Today, after I shared my angelic experience of the night before with Mary and Julie, Mary had to leave work. She had to think. To be alone. Her mind took what I had said and interpreted it in her way, a way that at first was painful and then, I think, I hope, healing. I did not like feeling I was in any way responsible for her pain and a part of me wanted to go into that feeling and dwell there and refuse to ever again take on the responsibility of asking for messages for others.

I really was stunned. It was one thing to get messages for myself. To get messages for another and to have them affect that person was different. Both Julie and Mary had been affected—one positively and one negatively. It threatened to overwhelm me.

But once begun, the messages of Peace became more important to me than anything else in my life. Our nightly conversations had grown to several pages in length and each covered a major issue affecting my life. The relevance of the Peace messages went beyond anything I had felt throughout the year from books that answered my questions or comforted me or supported my emerging beliefs. This was communication geared specifically to me and to my needs. And this was communication that seemed to come in words designed to get through to *me*. It was personal. I had a personal guide. I felt lucky beyond belief. How could I not be willing to share that guidance?

I concluded that the important lesson I had needed to learn from this experience was to be sure that I had permission, to always wait until I was specifically asked.

The concept of asking and being answered was still new to all of us, however. The angels seemed to suggest an ease to the process that none of us quite bought. If it were so easy, why had we not discovered it before? Why wasn't everyone doing it? And yet the things that are difficult in life tend to be the same things that are difficult in regards to spirituality. How many times do we want a hug from a spouse or sibling and not ask for it? How often do we need help and not request it, even of someone we know would be willing to give it? So not asking, then, appears to be a habitual human malady. Asking and being surprised at being granted a request also seems to be a typical state of affairs. So it was, in the beginning, with me and Peace. And so it was with each of us.

Mary was having a hard time asking. Not because Mary lacked faith but because Mary was afraid. Because there was only one thing she could ask. There was only one question.

Mary wanted what we all wanted. But she knew that first she had to get an answer to her question. And in order to get that answer, she had to lay her fear aside and ask. Her asking was an act of tremendous courage. That she asked her question of me and Peace, a tremendous honor.

She gave me a card the morning she asked. In it, she thanked me for sharing my spiritual journey with her and she thanked Peace. She thanked Peace before she even asked anything of him. And I knew she asked only what she had to know because she was desperate to know. She asked, "Is Grace all right?" On June 1, exactly one month after we had begun talking, Peace answered:

Mary has only asked because she has reached a point of being where she is ready to know, where she needs to know, where she must know. And I tell you, what Mary needs to know is this: she did everything right. She could not have loved more. She could not have felt more. She could not have withstood more than she did. She had the courage to trust in herself, in her intuition, and she was so right to do so. She was more than right in that there is no right and wrong in following our destiny. She did the only thing she could. And Grace did the only thing she could. Destiny is linked. Not only did Mary live her destiny and Grace live her destiny, but everyone else who was touched by Grace had Grace as part of their destiny, their road to travel, their bridge between the human and the divine. John, Amanda, Sara, the doctors, the nurses, people Mary doesn't even know. Wives, husbands, friends, daughters who heard of Grace's valiant struggle had their destinies touched by Grace.

And Grace, who Mary worried over so, was a being of pure love and pure light. She was all angel. We all have our angelness with us when we are born. We all have a wisdom unrecognizable in the human world. It is the wisdom of remembering. And Grace never forgot! She never forgot for a moment that she was a being of love, a being of one-ness. She knew exactly what she came back to the human form to learn:

Love. And she learned it. She learned it so fast and gave it back to the world so fast, there was no need for her to remain in human form. She never spent a moment on this planet when she was not sure, absolutely sure that she was a being of love. Why? Because she lived such a short life? That is part of the reason. The other reason was that she lived her entire life surrounded by love. She did not see tubes or surgical instruments as anything but what they were—instruments of love. She did not see nurses and doctors, she saw beings of love. And because she was wise with the wisdom of remembering, she saw her parents with perfect love. She saw them as the angels they are. She did not see one single imperfection because there was none to see.

Tell Mary that Grace remembered! She left this world a being of light just as she entered it. She had everything you seek! Everything Mary seeks! Why do you suppose she affected people so? They were in the presence of an angel, an angel who never forgot. One who could have turned around and left for home immediately, but who stayed to feel the love around her and to fill those around her with her divine love. Is Grace all right? No one could be better than Grace. Grace Is in divine oneness and love.

Thank you, Peace. I think I can rest assured that you have given Mary what she had to have—understanding and Peace. Thank you. Can I ask one thing more? As you know, ever since Grace, through Grace, because of Grace, Mary has been on a journey of her own. Similar to mine but unique to her. Her own spiritual quest. There have been times on this path when she has been certain Grace spoke with her through her computer. Sometimes the messages have been clear and sometimes they have not been. Sometimes it simply seems as if everything is a frustrating puzzle, as if the computer has gone haywire. She wants to write, she wants to communicate, but she is not only confronted with puzzles, but with an inability to go into her computer and write to her daughter. Can you tell her anything that will help her understand what is happening? Can you give her any assurance about how to know when Grace is reaching out to her? Can you help to solve the riddle?

What Mary has received is a reflection of herself. Of her state of being in the Now. Mary has lived through the greatest challenge that humans can face. And she has turned from that challenge, not with bitterness or anger, although these feelings at times fly across her Now, but with hope. What is her hope about? Finding the love she had with Grace. She was so full of Gracie's love that Gracie's loss felt like a great and awful emptiness, an emptiness so great and vast she wasn't sure she was alive. Wasn't sure she could live. How could Grace not return to comfort her and give her hope? How could Grace not return to help her on her journey? Grace is with her every step of the way. Grace leads her to the books, the birds, the signs, the flowers. Grace in her infinite, loving oneness knows the quickest route to welcoming Mary to be with her again.

Why does that way seem full of puzzles and frustrations? Because Mary is full of puzzles and frustrations. This is not something negative I am saying here. I am saying Mary lived through the greatest challenge a human can face and came out of it not with overwhelming anger and bitterness and despair, but with puzzles and riddles. Hurrah for Mary. Because Grace helped her back to remembering more than she has any concept of, she is in a state of puzzles and frustrations. She knows, Knows, more than she ever knew before. She is closer to oneness, closer to her angelhood, closer to the divine all-that-is than in any life-time. Yet that Knowing is hidden from her, much like a name you say is on the "tip of your tongue." It is not Grace, or Mary's angel, or anyone but Mary who keeps her in the state of frustration.

Again, this is not negative. For most humans, enlightenment is a lifelong occupation. There is a reason for that. There is a reason I only answer the questions you are ready to ask. There is a reason Mary is accessing all that she Knows in a slow and seemingly frustrating way. That reason Is. Like Mary Is. In the Now of life on this planet, Mary must function day to day: Mary works, Mary interacts with her family, Mary sleeps and dreams and walks and gardens. Perhaps Mary knows that knowing all that Is would make this impossible for her. For the here and now, Mary is wise enough to ask for only that which she can live with in the Now. But it is all there—on the tip of her tongue!

Why does it seem as if she is asking and searching and not being answered?

Because Mary is in a state of profound forgetting—something she needed to do in order to live with the truth of Gracie's life and death. In your human experience of time, it has been an eternity for Mary since Gracie's death—and an instant. But Mary is not alone. She will never be alone. Ask Mary what she loved about Gracie. Was it her infant face? Her body? Her fingers and toes? Her hair, her eyes? It was everything. And everything Gracie was was love. Pure love. And Mary will never be without it again. No amount of forgetting will rid her of it. There is nothing she can do and nothing she can be that will not carry Grace's love. At this time, it seems a small substitute for the child Mary longed to hold and bring home, but let me tell you, there is nothing greater than this love. Mary is blessed with this love. Mary has touched the divine.

I know these are not the answers in the form you would seek them to be. You want to know if Grace has communicated through the computer? Grace has communicated through love. You want to know what puzzles the computer represents. I tell you the computer represents Mary's puzzlement. You want to know how Mary can communicate. Through love.

All I can tell you is that Gracie is showing Mary the way. How does Mary know that Grace has not just taught her the lesson of asking for help? How does Mary know that This is not more important in the Now than something Grace might have communicated through the computer? If Mary will trust Grace to lead her to the keys, she will eventually be able to unlock all the doors.

Thank you, Peace. Is there anything else Mary should know now?

Tell Mary that she is all right. Tell Mary that everything she does is all right. Tell Mary that Grace and I are smiling.

XIV

DOUBT

The writing I did for Mary brought on a bout of physical, emotional, and psychic illness.

When I handed Mary the Grace message, I knew it became hers. I could not say, "Here it is, but don't show it to anyone. You can have it, but don't tell anyone where it came from. Don't tell them it came from an angel or that it was me who received the message." I couldn't say those things but I wanted to. Mary shared Peace's message with her husband, John, and I thought, *How will I ever show my face around him again? He will think I'm nuts.* She showed it to her mother, this woman whom I admired and who admired me, and I thought, *There goes that relationship.*

I felt horrendously exposed. I hadn't yet told anyone I was on a spiritual quest. And here were people who did not, could not, understand being told about the culmination of that quest. How could they understand without knowing what had led up to it? How could they take it, and me, seriously? And how evil would they think I was if they thought I was trying to deceive someone in a state of grief?

Before my journey with the spirit sisters began, I had been feeling a profound sense of isolation. Things were going well for me for perhaps the first time in my life. Because of this, I had begun to turn inward. I had a lot of internal things going on that I wanted to talk about, but all of my friends had needs that far exceeded my own. My sister was going through a divorce. Mary had lost a child. Another friend had taken her grandchildren into her home. Everyone had concerns that I could not compete with. By the time I began sharing with the spirit sisters, I was ready to bust. Months and months of thoughts and feelings were bottled up inside with nowhere to go. Once I began sharing with the spirit sisters, however, I realized I had not just been withholding for months—I had been withholding all my life.

After giving Mary the Grace message, I returned to that feeling of isolation. And I became terrified. I wanted connection with other people—not something that would isolate me further, not something else that would separate me, make me different. I was overwhelmed with a feeling of vulnerability. It was similar to the feeling I had experienced when I first opened my heart, but extremely magnified.

I realized that if I had spent my whole life holding myself in, withholding, and if now I was all right out there, visible, even if only to myself, I would naturally feel anxiety and imbalance. I knew it would have helped if I could have talked about it. But once again, I couldn't. Once again I was bottled up. Because the only people I could talk to were Mary and Julie, and I didn't want to say or do anything that would taint Mary's joy in Peace's message.

I even wondered for a day if I could talk to Peace. Because I had begun to doubt.

Finally, I wrote about my dilemma:

June 3, 1995

Yesterday was Donny's forty-first birthday and the day Uncle Nino died. And, just possibly, it was a day of rebirth for Mary and Grace. All three events (three again) were disturbing to me. Donny's birthday because he is at odds with his family. Uncle Nino because I mourn his passing and rejoice in it at the same time. And finally, there is Mary, and having shared my experience with her, felt her pain, felt her thanks, felt, too, her uncertainty and my own, I doubted myself, doubted Peace, felt right out there, tender and vulnerable with my feelings.

Wondering, *What if it came from me?* Wondering if I'm a fraud. Wondering if this whole business is suspect. Fearful, fearful in a loving world.

Help me, Peace. I have had a crisis of confidence. How can this be so after the gift you gave me? How can I be strong enough to own up to what is happening—to face the scorn of nonbelievers. And why have I opened myself for this? I have felt ill and shaken, as if my balance is off. If I cannot come to you with my doubts, whom can I come to? Can you tell me what is happening to me? I am sick and I'm afraid it is all one—this sickness and my doubt. If I have doubts, how can others not? And if they have doubts about my credibility, it takes from me everything I have worked for, attained. Because it means doubting me at some basic, soulful level. And I know others doubt. I'm only talking about a few people here, Peace. I'm hearing the word *trust* in my head.

How did Mary feel when she said Grace talked to her through the computer? She was sure and then she wasn't sure. You were sure and had your doubts. Yet by talking about it, it became acceptable truth. TRUTH. See how closely truth and trust are linked as symbols for you. It is no wonder that when you doubt you are being truthful, you doubt you can trust. Did your doubt in Mary's beliefs cause you to doubt her as a person? To doubt her integrity? No. But you are saying to yourself that it is different with you because you presumed to speak the truth about another to another. This is true. Truth. You got what you asked for, Margaret. So you immediately think, be careful what you ask

136

for. In a way, yes. As I am careful what I answer. But don't set your-self up with another set of rules. Follow your instincts. If asking for others makes you more fearful than helping others gives you joy, then do not ask for others. Trust your instinct to be your guide.

It's not that I don't want to share your guidance. It's that once I let what you give me out into the world it is not mine anymore.

Like all your writing and it is your primal fear. Can you not honor it and let it go?

Maybe not. I'm not sure. This is different.

Is it? Dear Margaret, it is not different to me. In oneness all things come from the same source.

It might be different if everyone realized that, Peace, but it feels to me like telling people apples are carrots.

Does it really? Or are you merely fearful people will take your apples and turn them into carrots?

Peace, I wanted so much what you have given me—to help me help myself, to go new to the new home, to go new into life. I didn't bargain for this other.

Bargain is a word of commerce. One of those words you want to leave out of your feelings, remember. Remember me? I'm not here to hurt you or to frighten you. You are frightening yourself by predicting horrible things for your future. You said yourself, the knowledge has only been shared with a few. I am not asking you to share it more widely than feels appropriate for you. Give yourself permission to be imperfect.

Jesus' apostles denied him. You do not have to rush out into the world and proclaim me. You do not have to give permission for the others you trust sharing with to share with others.

But I can't give something like I gave to Mary and say, "Keep it a secret."

Why can't you?

Because it wouldn't be right?

Right for whom? You cannot judge Mary's right nor she yours. You can only be what you are. If this is part of what you are, it is part of what you are. The choice for public or private is up to you.

But I already made a choice to share, albeit a limited choice. Now I feel powerless to control it.

You cannot control it. You can control very little in your world. I tell you, this is part of the same fear you had about your other writing, the fear of being known. And where does the fear of being known come from? The fear that what you are is not lovable. What in anything you have done makes you unlovable?

What if it makes me a lovable freak? a fool?

Fear of humiliation. Know your fears and practice releasing them.

Why am I adding fears at a time when I want to subtract them?

You have asked to be in the forefront of a movement that is sweeping the world. Those in the forefront are always conscious of those trailing behind. Will they scorn and snicker? If they do, they do so out of fear.

Love them and their fear will fall away. Their scorn and snickers will be just another part of the costume they wear.

I might know all of this, Peace, but I don't think it makes things any easier.

Easy is part of a concept that is essentially false. You are on a journey. You have been on journeys before. You take a trip and the obstacles along the way become the fond memories of tomorrow. Why? Simply because they were. Can you control what will be? No. So you must try to be in the now with love. I know you have heard it many times now and you think, that is Peace's answer for everything. You're right. It IS.

Peace, this has all been acceptable with Mary and Julie because they have been part of the process. Then we hear about others who are going through similar processes and we get excited because we are not alone, and so the whole thing has more validity and we read things that validate even more. But people like Donny, people in my family, I cannot imagine them understanding.

You give them little choice. You give them so little of yourself. I am only a small part of what you withhold.

I know. But suddenly you have become a huge part.

It is so for others too. And as long as they are afraid, the darkness will continue. Fear is the greatest obstacle to overcome. You are expecting a lot of yourself to expect you can turn away fear so quickly. You turn it away for moments at a time, for moments when you are in the now with love. Let those moments grow.

If you were visited by your Uncle Nino tonight, wouldn't that be a gift? Wouldn't you want to share it——to tell people? Haven't you listened to others tell of meetings with the deceased and thought them lucky? And yet there would be part of you that would doubt your visit from your uncle and that would doubt another's experience as well. But only a part. Another part would see luck, would see divineness. That is the duality you are a part of.

Know what you seek, Margaret. Knowing the duality will not necessarily make life easier and it will quite likely make life more complex. But the duality exists and you know it exists, have known it for a long time. Will saying you are afraid of it make it go away like monsters under the bed? Being afraid of it will only allow the shadow side to grow. Loving it will bring out the light. You have felt this. You have felt the lightness of being. Give yourself space to integrate what you have learned. Accept what IS. Love yourself. Trust yourself. Easy for me to say, I know. But what is the alternative?

Okay, Peace. Help me rest well? Help me sleep on it tonight and feel better in the morning?

I will always help, dear one. With whatever you ask of me.

What helped me through this time more than anything was the flow of daily life. My daughter graduated from high school a few days later. I was busy at work. Busy at home. I tried to just ignore my fear for a while longer and go on the way I had been.

Yet even while I continued to talk to Peace, I knew I needed, somehow, to place the messages in a larger context, a context from which I could learn to better understand them, to admit to them, and finally to share them. Help in doing this came from an unexpected source.

A Sunday-morning conversation between my husband and my son caused me to begin to look at Peace as a more natural part of my religious and spiritual life.

On that morning, my son had announced that he did not want to go to church because he did not believe in God. My husband told him that whether he believed in God or not was irrelevant; he still needed to go to church. Donny went on to talk about how he would often be consumed with a problem or worried about some situation when he went to church and how, after that quiet hour of contemplation, he would have a solution or just feel more peaceful about whatever was bothering him. He told my son, "I don't know if it's God or having a quiet hour, but I know that going to church is beneficial."

What Donny's comment did was help me change my perspective. It helped me look at conversing with Peace as a quiet hour, as just another form of prayer, as a tool that was beneficial in helping me solve my problems and feel more peaceful.

Over the coming months, I thought of all the people in the world going to church, going to the quiet, turning to prayer. It made me think of the Rosary and the repetition of those prayers said as one fingered beads, the whole process, it seemed to me now, one of turning off the conscious mind so that a still, quiet voice could be heard. It

141

didn't matter whether it was called prayer in one culture—one religion—meditation in another. It didn't matter whether people called that still, quiet voice that would come and make them feel better their own higher wisdom, or God, or an angel. It didn't matter whether they heard a voice at all.

But I imagined that if, after people prayed, after they went to church, after they meditated, they wrote down their thoughts, their feelings, their questions and the answers that had come to them, that it would be a lot like what I was doing. Saying the Rosary was a means of getting to that still, quiet voice in us just as my talking to Peace was.

Everyone thought the power was in the tool. Some would believe the power of one tool, such as the Rosary, to be more legitimate than that of another tool, such as the computer. But the power was in *us,* not the tool, as Peace would tell me when I was ready for a more philosophical look at the matter:

You worried, when you asked for Mary and Julie about the power of being a channel and about the responsibility. Think instead of the beauty, the symmetry, the flow of it. Honor it. Be grateful for it. Pray. It is a flow. From you to me, from me to you, but both at the same time. Like a river flows, always there and always moving, a place, an idea, a movement. Like thoughts that can't be grasped or proven but surely are. The channel is always open, dearest. You can block the flow but you cannot stop it. Moving with it is the safest, surest way to navigate it. You are always there. It is always part of your actions from the simplest to the most complex. Transmissions. Transforming the mission as you move to fulfill your destiny.

Mary and Julie, too, would find their means of communication and would find that at times it led to doubt. But we had become part of the flow and we each found that moving with it was the surest way to navigate it.

XV

COMMUNICATION

By mid-June, both Mary and Julie had made contact with their angels. Mary, at first, just wrote down her thoughts, not crediting them to anyone but herself. But soon she was reaching out, addressing others as well. Her journal entry of June 15, 1995, was addressed to Dearest Angels and Gracie, my daughter. Her entry a few days later: Dearest Angels and Gracie, my angel. And it only continued from there:

June 20: Dearest Angels and Gracie and all that is,

July 16: Dearest Angels, Gracie my love, God—all the universe!

August 16: Dearest God, my Angels, and my wonderful Gracie!

September 22: Dearest Angels, Gracie, and the Wonderful, Beautiful Universe!

October 1: Dearest Angels, Trinity, my Gracie, dearest God, and the Wonderful Universe,

October 17: Dearest Trinity, Gracie my love, my dearest Angels, dearest God, and all the Wonderful Universe …

Obviously, Mary's faith, trust, belief, and ability to communicate were expanding over time.

Julie made her first attempt in May and heard her angel's name as Water. Her second entry came on June 19. She made two requests to Water in July and one each for August, September, November, and December. On two occasions she received no response. She despaired a bit at not having the access that Mary and I had. She continued to ask me to ask Peace for words when she really felt she needed them. But what we all began to learn was that words were not our only means of communication.

In one of my earliest conversations with Peace I brought up the music of the Moody Blues and how all of their music seemed to contain divine messages. He assured me that music was a means of delivering and receiving messages.

145

So when Julie heard the same song, such as U2's "I Still Haven't Found What I'm Looking For" or R.E.M.'s "Losing My Religion," every time she turned on the car radio for days at a time and lyrics corresponded to angel messages, she began to see that there were other ways in which her angel, Water, was attempting to reach her.

By the time of her second journal entry, she knew music was one of those ways and that it was going to be significant to her. She asked Water about it.

How does music fit with me? What does it mean for me to play music?

It means for you to release your soul. Music is like water through your veins, pulsing.

In her entry of November 21, 1995, she asked about a moving experience she had while in a museum in Milan, gazing at a picture of a woman playing a mandolin. Water responded:

It was about what you know and have always known. You are a musician. It is there, bubbling, flowing, waiting for you to say okay, let's go. Believe it.

Julie had two means of communicating in addition to her scanty written communication with Water. Neither were as easily understandable as the written word, but both were extremely powerful and often were combined. Those means of communication were music and dreams. Their messages, when examined, were just as insightful and instructive as those Mary and I received through writing, and on occasion, they coincided with our written messages. It was almost as if while Mary and I were addressing the angels, the angels were addressing Julie, initiating contact in whatever way they could, using every means available to communicate their messages to her.

In July, for instance, Julie awoke in a dream to the sound of the k. d. lang song "Constant Craving." It was so loud that she needed to get up, even though she didn't want to, to go turn it off. The lyrics, which are about knowing that there is something "more" to life, spoke of the exact concerns Julie was dealing with at the time.

Julie's messages were not received only through music and dreams however. One message was delivered by a young Asian man who knocked at our office door seeking directions. When he peered through one of the door's windows, Julie saw his face and knew immediately he was another poor soul looking for directions. We got them all the time. It was a big university and our building a complex combination of A, B, C, and D corridors. Julie had gone to the door reluctantly, but her reluctance changed the minute she looked at the young man. It was like doing a double take, that sensation you get when you might know someone but you're not sure. But it wasn't about whether she knew him. She didn't know him. Yet she trusted him. "There were no barriers between the two of us," Julie said. "And I couldn't understand how that could happen with a complete stranger."

Shortly afterward, she had a dream in which both water and music played a part. It began with Julie dancing the flamenco and then becoming self-conscious about it and worrying about making too much noise. It continued with sitting at a table with an Asian man she was attracted to and then spilling red wine and overreacting to spilling it. Finally, she went to look out through the wall of floor-length windows and noticed that the water level outside was above her head. She put her hands on the glass and could feel the water making the windows bow in and out. She feared that the pressure from the water would break the glass.

She awoke from this dream in the middle of the night and a series of thoughts about the dream's meaning came to her: "You let yourself go and then you start blocking, getting self-conscious. People make mistakes. It's okay to make mistakes." And then she started thinking about the real young man she had seen in the hall and a flurry of realizations washed over her: "Yes," she heard, "he was reflecting your beauty. Your love. You're okay. He was a mirror reflection."

Julie said later that both the dream and the incident with the young man would have seemed insignificant if it weren't for the underlying message, which, not unlike "suspend judgment," followed her throughout the year. That message was about reflection and exchange, a message that also came up several times in our written angel messages.

What the messages seemed to do, in whatever form they took, was to reinforce the life lessons we were learning. The life lesson Julie was trying to learn was that if she could only let go and let her real self be seen, she would find nothing but love reflected back to her. That it would become an exchange. If she gave of herself to others, others would give to her as well.

The messages were like patterns we had to find, puzzles that needed to be put together. An angel message, or a tune that was heard briefly at a significant time, or a dream whose meaning seemed almost within grasp would be the beginning of a theme. The angel would say "release" and the songs would all be about letting go. A dream would reveal a specific fear and then the lesson of dealing with that fear would unfold over the next few weeks.

Unfolding was a theme in more than one way. Several times Peace or Water asked that Julie remove that which was shielding her true nature from being seen. Then she had a dream, a part of which included taking off several bandannas from around her neck and several layers of sweaters.

But unfolding was really just another way of saying let your true self be seen and it will reflect back to you! It was part of the pattern, part of the unfolding lesson.

No matter how the messages were delivered, they were always complementary and never contradictory.

One of Julie's earliest and loveliest messengers was her daughter, Lucia, who asked her why she "did that thing with her face," that clenching of her teeth and tensing of all her muscles that pulled the line of her neck taut. And one morning, after Julie had a dream during which she said, "I want to be a fuzzy white rabbit crunching carrots in the grass and giggling," Lucia gave her a sticker of a white rabbit. She also, with the unerring wisdom of a child, told her mother things like, "You can do anything you want to do" and that she was beautiful. It was clear that one of the lessons Julie was to learn from her children was that she was a lovable person.

Julie wasn't alone in receiving messages in ways other than the written angel communication. Titles of Beatles songs, such as "All You Need Is Love," often came to me out of nowhere. One day it was a John Lennon and Yoko Ono song, "(Just Like) Starting Over," that wouldn't leave my mind at a time when that phrase was particularly appropriate. And I remember clearly how a song came to me one day when I was walking out of work with Mary. Our cars were in different lots, and when we parted ways, the Stevie Wonder song "Isn't She Lovely," immediately entered my mind. One of my favorites occurred on a day on which I was feeling particularly good. I was walking to work with this tune in my head, and it took me several blocks before I could put words to it. The tune was from an old Budweiser commercial, and the words being put with it were, "You have it all, you have it all."

Mary and I also received messages from dreams occasionally; we often dreamed about one another, and Mary and Julie still occasionally shared dream images. Once, within weeks of each other, for instance, they each had a dream about huge angels filling the sky.

Only one further incident had the intensity of those that had come earlier in the year. This time, the event included both a dream and a vision.

It was on a Sunday afternoon in July that Amanda, Mary's stepdaughter, saw Grace. Amanda saw a one-year-old toddler sitting in a chair in the backyard. She wore a pink robe that had heart-shaped lockets on the tie and fur around its bottom. On her feet were moccasins with a moon and star on them. The baby had curly hair and fat cheeks. She was sitting before a pitcher of lemonade, scooping at it with her hands as if she were playing at drinking it. When she saw Amanda, she said, "Bye" in a high, faraway voice, and vanished into a white light Amanda called "brighter than the sun."

On that same Sunday night, Julie was dreaming. It was one of those rainy, dark nights (in the dream), but Julie opened her front door. Right outside, on the porch, was one little moccasin and it was wet around it.

It was obvious by this time that our children, husbands, strangers on the street, all could be messengers now that we were open to receiving their messages.

We knew that, in whatever form and through whatever means, the lessons were all important. Once again, communication itself had a dual meaning: if we hadn't been bringing the "messages" we received forth, talking about them, sharing them, pooling our resources to decipher and understand them, the messages might have just become thoughts that came and went from our minds, as transitory and fleeting as one usually thinks of a dream being. And if they hadn't seemed important, we might have been content to let this be so. But when we shared them, sometimes hesitantly, shyly, saying things like, "I'm sure this doesn't mean anything but . . ." one of us would see the importance behind the image, lyric, dream, thought. Without "suspend judgment," we might not have learned forgiveness. Without the repeated messages concerning revealing herself, Julie might never have come to believe she had qualities within that were worth revealing. Without Julie bringing in the Emmanuel books, I might not have ever attempted to talk to my angel. (Even though *Ask Your Angels* assured me that I could communicate, it was the Emmanuel books that made me want to.) If I had not contacted my angel, Mary has assured me, she never would have tried to contact hers. One communication led to another, led to another. It was an exchange and the exchange seemed to have a ripple effect.

The very goodness of the communications told us that what was happening was worth taking note of. There was never, during the entire course of the year, a dream that said, "Shame on you." Never once did the lyrics that repeated in our minds, or on the radio until we noticed them, speak of anything negative. Was it our state of mind creating the messages or the messages creating our state of mind? We didn't know. But if one could "suspend judgment" long enough to believe in angels, why should the means of the angel messages be judged? And if the messages themselves were repeated in several different formats, wasn't that just calling our attention to their importance?

.

XVI

FLOW

Our spiritual quest had moved to a higher plane. We had gone beyond the ordinary and yet we were still ordinary women. Perhaps because we had gone beyond the ordinary, perhaps because for a time, everything felt important, significant, we fell back upon the ordinary in the same way one takes comfort from a familiar place, a comfortable pair of slippers. Routine, after this break from the routine, felt good. And rather than asking of us extraordinary things, our spiritual quest returned to the ordinary with us. It joined us in our ordinary lives. It began by asking us to be present in the now.

Mary actually bought a watch that had the word *now* on its face. I quit wearing my watch altogether. We realized we had flexibility, or flow, in our lives. And with this realization, our days took on more depth and time became more fluid.

Mornings that used to be a rush became lovely times to experience the Now. Mary rearranged her daily schedule so she could have her morning coffee on her back steps. I took a new route to work, avoiding the freeway and enjoying instead the trees along one of my city's grand avenues, the view of the river.

Julie came in one morning talking about a pair of new white socks that had been sitting in her drawer for a long time. She talked about them because she saw how they were an allegory for her life. Because she had been *saving* them—as it seemed she had been saving what was best in herself. This saving was the opposite of the phrase "There's no time like the present." For Julie, there was "no time like the future." After talking about it, after seeing what she had been doing, Julie came in proudly wearing the new white socks. She wasn't saving anymore. She was becoming present.

We heard birdsong, saw flowers and clouds, appreciated the feel of the sun on our skin, the breeze in the air. We remembered to breathe. People smiled at us. Had they been doing that all along and we hadn't noticed, or was there something new in our faces, something that invited smiles? Every song on the radio spoke of love to Mary and me, of water to Julie. Where had these songs come from? Old and new, they were new to us. Because we *heard* them.

We worked in what is referred to as the health sciences area of the university. My husband, after visiting once, remarked, "I didn't expect it to be so sterile." But sterile is what it is. The health sciences buildings are on a street lined by dormitories and parking ramps, a street known for its wind-tunnel effect as it snakes between the health sciences towers to the dead-end circle at the front of our building, the former hospital. The area does not have the avant-garde casualness of the university's West Bank campus across the river from us or the grand educational feel of the main East Bank mall lined with its old trees. We imagined that it had more of a corporate-America atmosphere than any of the other areas of the university. Even the people seemed to be different here. There were few of the body-pierced, dyed-hair nonconformists one saw hanging around the art and political science and literature buildings. Health-professions students seemed freshly scrubbed and conservative, their professors freshly scrubbed and conservative and older. There seemed to be a preponderance of civil service women in nylons, high heels, and polyester skirts, a preponderance of white men in suits.

When, in the spring of the year of the births, our

department was moved from offices in the main corridor of the old hospital building to cubes in a far corner on a lower floor, it hadn't been our decision. It was a political decision and our program had little political clout. We moved under protest to the smaller quarters. Only later did we see how the move enhanced our own movement. The private offices of old would not have been conducive to the sharing that went on. The old office with its steady interruptions would not have provided the privacy we came to rely on. The isolated work space became a facilitator of our journey, our haven.

Without knowing how important it would come to be, we established the three members of our team in one room, the remaining office staff, sometimes numbering three, sometimes four, in the other. We positioned our cubicles as best we could around the room's two windows, faced our desks away from each other so that telephone conversations could take place with some hint of privacy, gave our large wooden conference table away and replaced it with a small, round, pink Formica one that would fit the remaining space, and we were back in business: I in the middle cubicle, Mary to my left, and Julie to my right.

We would begin our day joining in the little room we had designed as best we could with our mishmash of office furniture and files and modules. We had too much stuff for too little space. Besides the desks, the files, the computers, the copier, the fax, our office had artifacts. Our students came from around the world and each came bearing gifts, gifts that were on display in every nook and cranny that wasn't filled with office paraphernalia.

Because we had no offices, no doors, we made doorways out of our modules, and it was in these doorways that we gathered to begin our workday. We called our first-thing-in-the-morning talks our "morning update," which became as habitual as picking up the mail. We had been apart for a dozen hours or a weekend and what we did or felt or read during those hours was now brought to the others for exploration. We would begin by hearing one another's dreams, often pulling out a dictionary to discover the hidden meanings behind a dream image, symbol, or word. Then we would hear about any reading one of the others had done, learn of any angelic messages, signs, or feelings. Learn, too, about what was going on in each other's families. Our morning update complete, we would then wander off three or four feet to our little cubicles and work until my mid-morning cigarette break.

Most mornings, except in winter, Mary and Julie would join me for my break, appropriately, on Church Street. If it was cool, we would stand beneath the entryway arch or sit on the steps. In nice weather we walked across the street to where the sun lit on windowsills large enough for the three of us to sit on together, and there we would continue the conversation of the morning.

Often we would lunch together, either at the little conference table in our area or at a nearby restaurant, the Big

Ten. Having read in *A Course in Miracles* that we should ask the Holy Spirit to make all of our relationships holy, we asked in a booth at the Big Ten over turkey sandwiches that He bless the relationship the three of us shared. It was also in the Big Ten that Mary had an epiphany concerning her humanness, and it was here, in the midst of blaring music and lunch crowds, that we often came to new awareness about matters of concern to us.

Mary had begun to carry a "spirit bag," a briefcase in which she toted her dream journal and any books we were discussing. Often the spirit bag came with us to the Big Ten. With a whole lunch hour at our disposal, we could read each other important passages from books or angelic messages, or discuss a dream or message in more depth.

It was a giddy time. A fun time. Everything had meaning: colors, stones, bumper stickers, clothing, jewelry. Everything was a message. A bad day was no longer just a bad day. Having a bad day occasionally may have been normal once, but no longer. Now a bad day was a message. It had something to tell us. An aching back was no longer something to be put up with. It was a message. It had something to tell us.

Our wardrobes were suddenly all wrong. Where were the flowing fabrics? The cotton? The natural fibers that would feel good against the skin, that would move with the breeze? Mary started growing her hair out because she wanted flowy hair. I quit drying and setting and pulling mine off my face with clips, and let it be natural.

We began to tease Julie about the knot in her brow, the tension that pulled the veins and muscles of her neck into taut strings. We could tease her, we could notice, because they were no longer constant. She could be seen, occasionally, to look relaxed. She began to glow with a light that seemed to come from within. I quit taking my medication for my fibromyalgia and I was fine. The muscles that had been tight for more than five years finally relaxed.

People began to remark that we had changed.

Our secretary, Felicia, used to tease me about how little I expressed myself—about anything. I would come in and share some news about something really great, buying a new car, for instance, and she would say, sarcastically, "Gee, I'm glad I can tell you're so happy about it!" Now she was beginning to be able to tell how I felt about things—good and bad. She even remarked about how I touched her arm one day. I had been so standoffish previously that a simple touch on the arm, a touch of understanding, was noteworthy.

Our internal changes were being reflected externally! How could they not? Some things were easily seen, such as my change of clothing, from form-fitting business suits to flowy dresses, my more relaxed way of wearing my hair, my softer makeup. Mary, too, changed her clothing. She no longer needed things to match, but to have meaning. She became a body artist, finding jewelry especially that spoke to her, that proclaimed who she was or who she was becoming. Julie, who had always agonized over spending seven dollars on a skirt at a consignment store, bought and wore daily a forty-dollar necklace that she felt symbolized outwardly the changes that were occurring inwardly.

We stopped reading the newspaper and hardly watched television. It was no longer acceptable to submit ourselves to violence. We just couldn't take it. We realized we didn't have to. We were becoming open and, in our opened states, vulnerable. Vulnerable to good and vulnerable to bad as well. We started experimenting, led by Mary's reading, with energy. We could turn off television violence, but could we turn off another's negative energy? Often the answer was yes!

In large part, people around us seemed to respond to our new personas. We may not have been talking about our dreams and angelic messages with our husbands and families, but we were, nonetheless, different with them.

Mary, who had always had control issues with her husband, John, just gave up trying to win control and reaped huge rewards. She realized that all the "division of labor" fights they used to have, in which she would become angry because she felt John wasn't pulling his weight, had been the result of her feeling *she* had to pull all the weight herself. The fights had been the result of her own feeling that the only way for her to be *good* was to be in control, to maintain what she had. And she had to maintain what she had perfectly. Everything in her home had needed to be in its proper place, perfectly coordinated, matching. It didn't matter that John would gladly have picked up his own clutter when he was done doing whatever he was doing. It mattered that he cluttered at all. It didn't matter that John would do what she had deemed "his chores" when he was ready to do them. If she was ready for them to be done, they had to get done—right then—and so she would do them herself.

She knew the ultimate change had occurred when John asked her, one day, when she was going to get around to doing the dishes and she responded, "When the spirit moves me." Even John laughed. What had ruffled her before—things out of place, things not done, things not perfect—were now signs of living going on, of love going on.

My husband, like Mary's, provides a good example of how my changes affected others. A man of keen wit and gentle wisdom, he is outwardly a gruff, working-class "man's man," a hunter, a fisherman, a man not readily prone to revealing feelings other than those he considers "manly"—like anger. Fiercely loyal, he expected others to be fiercely loyal, and if he felt betrayed, he held grudges. He had, in the past, gone for years without speaking to one family member or another over wrongs he had felt were done to him.

Two major family squabbles occurred during this time, both of which were large enough that in the past, he would have written off those family members with whom he argued. Now the fights were allowed to blow over.

One evening Donny told me about his day and how different it was from days he used to have. How before, if he had been on a ladder and dropped a hammer even once, he would get angry, swear, fume. And now he could drop a hammer, climb down and get it, climb back up, drop it again, and still not be upset. And he said he knew it was because of me. He didn't elaborate on why he thought I had anything to do with this. But I was thrilled! It was as if my new peacefulness was extending to him.

Another night he told me that I was at ease now, and so now he and everyone else in the family could be more at ease. It had been the perfect word choice. I thought about Thomas Moore's definition of *dis-ease,* and concluded, "That is what I used to have. I was so full of dis-ease it might as well have been an illness."

We were becoming unified in our marriage. What had previously been "his" church and "his" family was gradually becoming mine as well. Donny's nephews were no longer "his" nephews and mine, "mine." His nephews were the same little boys they had always been, but now I suddenly loved them like my own, as if they were part of me, because they were. And as subtle as these changes were, they were noticed. I was treated more like one of the family—both by the family of my husband and of my church—because I was.

I felt some of the biggest rewards within my family were those that came from slowing down and, in slowing down, no longer resenting the small demands others made on me. When I slowed down, I was no longer uptight all the time. I made the choice to slow down when the spiritual lessons I had been learning came nose-to-nose with a life lesson one morning.

I had been on my way out to work when I found my daughter Mia's car parked behind mine in the driveway. I was furious. I was in a hurry. I woke Mia from a sound sleep and demanded that she immediately move her car out of my way. I sat impatiently in my car, watching as she came out in her pajamas and shoes, bleary-eyed and stumbling, and then found that the car wouldn't start. I listened to the car whine and whir, watched my daughter's frustration grow as she tried it again and again. But I was in too much of a hurry to have any compassion for her. I hopped out of my car and demanded that she put the car in neutral. With the strength of my impatience, I pushed the car down the driveway and out of my way. As I drove out past her, I saw my husband coming out the door of the house. He would take care of it.

But I hadn't even gone a block before I felt absolutely horrible. What was the matter with me? What did five minutes one way or the other matter? If I had calmly gotten Mia's keys and moved the car myself, the car probably would have started just fine. She had probably flooded it because I had made her so nervous. My impatience had led to a rotten start of the day for me, for Mia, and now probably for Donny as well.

What hit me as I drove on to work was the teaching,

164

"Act from love and you cannot act wrong." I had been too impatient to remember love, too much in a hurry. I had forgotten to love and now I, and others, would suffer for it the rest of the day. I vowed it wouldn't happen again and it didn't. Because the thing was, it wasn't about minutes, it was about love. And this was clearest, most evident, in the little things. The little things that add up to make life hellish or heavenly. In a hundred little ways each day, we each have the choice of acting from love or not.

Julie's theme of being the lucky one traveled through her marriage as well. Her husband, Kelly, who was affected by retinitis pigmentosa, or RP, a genetic degenerative retinal disease that causes blindness, was slowly losing his vision. What right did she have to complain or to make demands upon him when he was facing something so devastating? Consequently, she had always placed her own needs— from the simplest to the most important—last, if she had let them be known at all. If she wanted to do something on the same night Kelly did, she gave up her activity in favor of his. If Kelly wanted to spend money in one way and she in another, she gave in. When he had wanted a career change and decided to start his own business, she went along even though the change terrified her on many levels, particularly financially. She had gone along even though she realized this change meant that she would always have to keep a job that provided the stable income and medical benefits the family still needed.

Even while Kelly's decisions and the changes they made in her life had been positive, she now felt as if she could have more of a voice in things. And this "coming to voice" was quite literal—as Mary and I saw in our conversations with Julie. Where we had both, in the past, often finished sentences for Julie because she just didn't seem to be able to find the words to do so herself, we were now seeing that she carried on. That she kept going until she got things out. She was coming to voice.

Now she was beginning to realize she could not keep holding all of her dreams and desires within. Now she saw that what she kept from her husband injured him as much as it injured her. Kelly did not want a woman who would sacrifice herself for him, but one who would accept him and accept herself, just as they were, without pretense, without withholding.

We weren't preaching what we were learning; we were living it, and it flowed into every area of our lives. Things went well for us. We were, quite simply, happier, and others were happier to be around us.

My husband and I didn't fight anymore. We sold a house, bought a house, had the usual, normal, ordinary problems with our teenage children, and we just dealt with them. And what was more, we recognized we weren't fighting anymore and were pleased. In a conversation one evening, Donny told me he thought it had become fashionable for people to complain, that people never used to complain about everything like they did now, and how he recognized that we weren't like that. We were happy. And he hoped our happiness would set an example for those around us.

Almost without realizing what we were doing, we had brought some of what we had in the office beyond the office. But the office, and our day-to-day interaction with one another, was still what was most important.

When Julie, Mary, and I were together at work, all of our emotions were given a place to be, and given that place they came. We were happier, but we cried often. We became emotional beings. We cried tears of happiness and tears of sadness. Some days we were drained by noon because we had laughed and cried so hard during the morning. I cried more in those months of discovery than I had in my entire adult life.

It is impossible now to remember what it was all about—all that laughter, all those tears. One thing simply seemed to lead to the next. It seemed as if every feeling we had, every thought, was universal. There was almost nothing we had experienced that one of the others had not experienced also. Everything was acceptable. We were not alone. We were not lonely!

Every day, every hour, someone brought something that another seemed to need. A bit of advice, a bit of humor, a bit of compassion.

There seemed to be an end, for brief periods of time, to

struggle of any sort. We could simply *be* in each other's presence. We could rest. Let down our guards, our defenses. It was a peaceful place. Like a stolen moment in time.

It seemed impossible that what was happening was happening. Not the big stuff so much as the little: the peace, the cessation of struggle, and the work getting done in the midst of it. I look back and wonder how we did it all. We were busy at work by this time. We did just as much as any other year. We scheduled faculty, produced curriculum, admitted students. We got it all done. We had it all! It was exhilarating and exhausting at once. We were aware every day of how lucky we were. And we talked, during this busy time, of what it would be like when we weren't as busy. It was so new. Everything was so new. Our days were so different. What would they be like when the busy season was over? It was almost too much to imagine. We didn't know if we could take anything more. There was a collective feeling of operating at our peak, of getting the most out of everything, of being in a time that would be impossible to top.

And in a way, it was. It was the beginning and had the energy of beginnings, of innocence, of exploration. We met each day with awe. By the end of the year, we were experimenting with saying "I believe it" instead of "I can't believe it" about everything. By the end of the year, the freshness of it had worn off a little bit. We were becoming used to it. We were beginning to believe it. But for now it was new and it didn't seem as if anything could be better.

In our program the end of spring quarter was the peak of the season, the home stretch, the eve of our students' arrival. All of our work during this time was teamwork, no one could take vacation; we had a common goal, deadlines, schedules to keep. In the midst of the increased pace, we began to look forward to routine tasks that had once been monotonous and dull, because they allowed our minds to be free. Mailings became causes of celebration because we could do them together—one labeling, one folding, one stuffing—producing while we talked, while we laughed, while we cried. There was a unity about the work that went beyond teamwork. We began to dream about a world in which we could work together toward a common goal that was our own, even while we were doing it! Even while we were in the midst of it, we voiced our concerns, one or another of us, that it would end someday, that we would go on to other endeavors that might not include each other.

There we were, three civil servants, working in a small office of a large institution where no one would believe, no one could imagine, what was going on. We said often, if someone had told us six months ago we would be happy about sitting down to a mailing so that we could talk about angels and our spiritual life, we would have said they were crazy. We would have said we would be crazy if this came to be. But it had come to be and we were not crazy. We were happy. We felt alive! We were present. We were integrated. We brought to work all that we were in a pure, raw form. We became our true selves when we were at work.

Our days had reversed themselves. Now we could hardly wait to get to work so we could be who we were, and when we left for our homes at the end of the day, we often felt we left our best selves behind. When we left, we took on our other roles. We became wives and mothers and daughters again. We did our ordinary things—went grocery shopping and picked up the dry cleaning and went to the bank. We gassed our cars, washed our clothes, read our mail, and paid our bills. But these activities no longer felt like "real life."

It was nice that I was more at ease in my home environment, that Mary was less controlling, that Julie was coming to voice. But these things were all offshoots of the journey, not the journey itself. We were grateful for these benefits, these by-products, but we knew we still needed each other and the office environment for our journey to continue. We didn't want to let the distractions of our work and our ordinary lives halt our progress toward our real lives and our real selves.

In the office, everything was fuel for our fire. But we *were* the fire. We were finding the something more we had sought all along and it was *us.* It was what we had when we were together.

What went on in the office between the three of us felt like real life. It was as if while we were there, while we were together, we "got it." We knew what it was all about. It was why we started to dream up schemes of working together forever. How could we possibly repeat the string of events that had brought us to where we were? It felt like a once-in-a-lifetime, unrepeatable occurrence. It felt unique to the three of us and to that time and place.

It was a time when we would gladly have brought in cots and set up residence. It was a time that felt too good to be true. It was a time that had to end.

It was the honeymoon, the fairy tale, the dawning of the quest, the start of the adventure. It had to face the test of that other life, that life we no longer thought of as real life. It had to face the reality of our move out of our office to the conference center where we ran our summer program. It had to face the test of "after the students were gone" vacations. It had to move with us or we would lose it. And it had to do more than that. Unless it could become more than a side benefit in our ordinary lives, it would become a fantasy, a fairy tale in which we would not live happily ever after. Because we didn't live in our cubicles in our tiny office in our large institution. Because we couldn't bring in our cots and our toothbrushes. What we had found was meant to go with us into our lives. It was meant to be more than a by-product that made life easier. It was meant to *be* our lives.

XVII

PREPARING

We were still, however, not quite ready. In June, as my daughter Mia was about to graduate from high school, Peace had taught me the lesson, "know for what it is that you prepare." I had been busy with work, busy with my spiritual quest, busy getting ready to sell my home. Planning for Mia's graduation and all the related activities had felt like a burden until Peace reminded me to be aware for what it was that I prepared. I was preparing to send my daughter into the next phase of her life, the life of a young adult. I was about to honor all that she was and all that she hoped to become. I was preparing to honor all that was possible for her. The limitless possibilities of her future. The graduation planning ceased to be a burden. And the thought of "being aware of what it was that I prepared for" stayed with me through my days, as "suspend judgment" did.

Julie, Mary, and I had been preparing to go out into the world new, as my daughter went out into the world new. In July, leaving the office was thrust upon us just as leaving high school was thrust upon my daughter a month earlier. It did not mean that we were ready. We were, in fact, still preparing. As my daughter was still preparing.

What was new was the sense of limitless possibility, the sense of becoming. New, appropriately, for my daughter. New, because of the spiritual quest for us ordinary women well beyond the years of growing up, well beyond thinking our possibilities were limitless. We had a sense of something awaiting us.

And at the same time we sensed we were putting something behind us. It was July again. The month of the births. Peter would have his first birthday.

It became a time to get through so that we could go on. What awaited seemed to be on the other side of July, on the other side of August. Waiting beyond the busy season, my move, the birthday, the anniversary of the death. Waiting for the time we would be together again in the office. Waiting for the three to gather in what had become our holy place. We had become dependent. And we fought that. We reasserted our independence. We became individuals again.

There were times during our "on-campus" sessions when we were able to use what we had learned thus far. We no longer expected crisis. We experienced a new sense that what will be, will be. That what needed to get done would get done. That there was no need to panic. When a problem arose, the point was to solve the problem and go on rather than to dwell in the problem and give it control over us. When things needed to get done, we did them. I remember winding extension cords from audio-visual equipment at the end of a long day and, instead of resenting the task, enjoying the quiet of the moment, enjoying the act of forming it into circles with my hands. There were times when we remembered to be in the now even while waiting for the now to be over.

But there were also times when we forgot. The biggest stresses came when we tried to re-create what we had in the office by taking ourselves away for a long lunch or a short break, when we tried to create artificially what had come naturally in another time and space. We were going to bring what we had learned into the world, but we weren't going to be able to bring the world of the office with us. What we had in the office was going to have to transform.

There was a hint of melancholy, of mourning, about this time, even while we prepared for the limitless possibilities that were coming. I was eager to move into my new home at the same time that I was feeling sentimental about the old. Julie was eager to celebrate Peter's birthday and wistful for a year that had gone by too quickly. Mary was eager to put the year of her daughter's death behind her and yet resentful of the healing properties of time.

We were eager and reluctant both.

And so we struggled once again. We had good days and bad. We weren't always crazy about each other. We would arrive at our conference center by 7 A.M., set up for 8 A.M. classes, break down after classes were over at 5 P.M., and then prepare for social activities or evening sessions, sometimes stretching well into the night. After these long days, there were times when we would be grateful to get away from each other, when other things were more important. We felt ordinary again some days, separate most days. There wasn't time to read or write. There was hardly time to think. And so we concentrated on what would come later . . . after our work in July was over . . . after the vacations we would take in August were over.

For we all had our secret fears. We would get through this busy time, this work that had been our goal and our mission. We would get through the July and August anniversaries. We would come back from the vacations and we would join once again. We wondered if things would be the same. We wondered if things would be different. We knew we would go on to something more. We *knew* this. We knew we were preparing. But what we were preparing for remained a huge unknown.

XVIII

SURRENDER/LETTING GO

With the coming of September, we were back together with time stretching before us once again. We were back in the office. Back in our own little world. We were *back!* We greeted each other with enthusiasm. We had missed each other.

The cycle of a year different than our ordinary years was now complete. Mary had survived a whole year without her daughter. She had watched summer turn to fall, fall to winter, winter to spring, and spring to summer once again. Fall was upon us—again. That Grace had left Mary at the time the sun was waning, the gardens ending their growth cycle, the gloomier skies of fall approaching, had somehow seemed appropriate. That the fall of the following year would begin differently was a measure of the potency of the cycle. The year following the death of her daughter was behind her. She had survived! She had found she could go on living! Mary felt a burst of new energy. Something finally felt completed, and it seemed as if it might be the cycle of pain. It seemed as if it might be time to let go.

For me a different cycle was wrapping itself up. My move from the old house to the new was now complete. The move had long been an allegory to me, an outward representation of the change occurring within. I had known I would go new to the new home. I had prepared myself as I had prepared the old home for its sale. I had worked hard to shed those things I no longer needed. I had sorted and sifted, throwing some things away, putting a fresh perspective on others. I had left the old home with love and fell in love with the new. Peace had said: "Honor the old home. The new home will honor you." Perhaps he meant that home is within, a place of love and contentment, or he may have been speaking literally of the new building, the new structure. Because everything about the new home was a joy and everything went well. It truly seemed as if the new home honored me, blessed me. I, too, was full of a new energy. Released

177

from a time-consuming enterprise, I could settle into other pursuits, including my spiritual quest.

Julie approached the fall with impatience. She was tired, too, of the old self. She strove to define what blocked her from moving forward. She strove to let go. To quit letting those things she could not define hold her back. She strove to come into being.

We were back in the same familiar setting but we were different. More confident. We had survived being away from each other, survived a trip into the world, and we had carried many lessons we had learned there. Even if we could not carry the experience of the office into the rest of our lives, our lives could improve. We could bring with us the enthusiasm of the journey. We had left behind our mourning for what couldn't be and we were anxious to discover what could be. We had come back together and found that we still had much to learn from each other, found that the office still offered us a place to be while we were discovering what we would become.

We came back knowing we were each going to continue on our journey . . . even if it meant that our paths would diverge.

Yet it was more as if we were each in a different place on the same path, or perhaps we were heading in the same direction through different routes. Still sharing the spiritual journey yet living three separate spiritual journeys, learning to blend them with our three ordinary lives. Learning to let go of willfulness and to accept guidance on the journey from sources higher than ourselves.

My surrender/letting go had happened almost accidentally:

August 27, 1995

I am writing from my new office in my new home. It is in
a corner of a damp basement (if you can believe it, I let my
husband appropriate the sunroom for the TV) and I don't
care. It feels so good to be back. I sat down, pulled up the
file I now called Peace rather than Prayer, and there it
was. It felt almost miraculous to see it here, in this new
house. In this new house where everything has come
together so beautifully.

But this is the biggest, the grandest, the happiest. Peace
is here! I have read the whole Peace file, and I am moved
by it, by my own innocence more than my knowledge. I
haven't thought of myself as innocent since I was thir-
teen. There is a sweetness about the Peace file—from the
first day when I was told to smell the sweetness. It is the
sweetness of innocence, of teacher and pupil. To read it is
like learning to read all over again—the knowledge, the
excitement, the adventure. The love of words! I cannot
begin to say how much it all means to me.

And so, here I am, about to ask Peace to join me once
again, putting it off only so that I can wait until I have a
quiet hour with no pressure to do other things. Because I
know Peace is my still, quiet voice within and I know he

has led me and will continue to lead me to breakthrough moments of higher consciousness and greater creativity.

I have begun to say affirmations from a book I just bought, *Higher Creativity: Liberating the Unconscious for Breakthrough Insights,* by Willis Harman and Howard Rheingold. Those affirmations are

> I am not separate.
> I can trust.
> I can know.
> I am responsible.
> I am single-minded. I have no other desire than to know and follow the will of the deepest part of myself.[3]

And I realize that this is letting go. Turning events over to the higher self, the unconscious, surrendering, if you will, to the will of God.

And this is where I am. This is my beginning in my new home. Happily, contentedly, surrendering, letting go. What a relief!

I cannot wait any longer. Welcome Peace! Welcome back! Welcome home! It's me, calling you home. Will you answer?

I am here and I am happy to be with you. I am smiling. We are not Home, but we are home on earth, home in the physical, home in well-being. Safe, comfortable, surrounded by beauty. Home. Peace on Earth.

Thank you, Peace on Earth, for bringing Peace to my little piece of it. For bringing yourself here. This, too, is a relief. You're here! My eyes fill with tears of joy to have you here, to have what we have here continue. Thank you. Welcome.

You have learned much in our break.

I have tried (for want of a better word). I have been mainly involved in the physical, but as I said before, as it comes together it has risen to a higher level.

Yes! It has living spirit. Like the words that come together to form a beautiful philosophy, a living message. Everything is coming together.

Is it, Peace? Is everything?

Everything has come together for you to the point of trust. Why trust? Because you have decided to let go. No. Not decided. You have let go. With your innermost being you Know, you Trust that you can let go. I could not force it upon you with my words. You were the only one who could make the choice. And you did it now, today, on this time of our rejoining. Hurrah for you, dear one. You are one step, one giant step, one leap closer to Home.

I didn't even realize I was going to surrender until I did, until I had, and the relief flooded me. I think it was an unconscious decision as much as it was a conscious one. I think this is the way it is supposed to be.

That is the goal. To let go and let your highest self, your connection to all that is, do the planning, the deciding, the choosing for you. It is not

181

not you. It is the best you. It is us. It is from oneness. You and the all that is connected. Linked. Xed. Joined.

This is so new to me. Now what do I ask you, dearest Peace?

If surrendering has lulled your curiosity, it is only so that you can rest in the relief. Rest as you have never rested before. Rest, and in your resting will come the stirring of the still, quiet voice, the voice that asks for more out of a whisper of calmness rather than the raging of necessity, desperation, frustration.

I have no other desire than to know and follow the will of the deepest part of myself.

Look deeply and there I am, reflecting back what you are. . . .

Welcome to my new home, Peace. Thank you.

Rest in relief in your new home. That is all the thanks I ask.

On my first day back at work after the move, Julie very casually said that she had been thinking she just ought to ask me to ask Peace what the heck was wrong with her. She very humorously told of her steps backwards—the tension and gritting of the teeth, the strain she was under. Just as Mary had pantomimed "suspend judgment," she played the two sides of herself that were in conflict, one side constantly saying, "Yes I can," the other, "No I can't." And she asked: How do I get out from under it?

The answer I received, as so often happened, was very

simple. Condensed, it simply said, *Tell Julie to have a dialogue with herself. What is at the center of Julie? Who is she?* She was being asked to get to know herself. *Tell her I am aware that this is not new advice; not the timeless wisdom she seeks. But the timeless wisdom she seeks will be found on the journey inward.*

This message wasn't news. Few of the angel pronouncements were. As Peace told me early on, he wouldn't tell me anything I didn't already know. But, oh, how I wanted him to. How we all did.

We were back and we wanted More, More, More. We wanted answers. How could we proceed without direction? No matter how many times we were told to turn within for that direction, we still hoped for external answers. We looked to each other, we looked to the angels, and finally we looked to a spiritual retreat.

We were lucky enough to have access, through one of the professors with whom we worked, to a wonderful, secluded cabin not far from where we lived. We had used the cabin before for work retreats. Now we sought to use it for a spiritual retreat. We wondered again, What would happen if we had "real" time together. If we could get away from it all. If we didn't have to work while we were together. Our fantasy had changed from one in which we would work together for the rest of our lives to one in which we could just *be* together.

I wrote to Peace about my expectations before the big event, saying: "I want things to grow around me and to become more than what they have been. With the spirit

183

sisters, Peace, I truly feel that anything can happen. That if we go about it right, the possibilities are limitless. With the spirit sisters, Peace, I feel hope for myself."

Our yearning was so poignant, really. We were all expectant, we just did not know of what.

Mary had begun her search because death wasn't good enough; it had no meaning for her. She had not asked for and had not wanted to experience any of the unusual things she had encountered in her grief and her recovery from that grief. She went resistingly, as she had resisted getting an unsolicited message from Peace. Mary asked only for what she had to know. She was on this journey to find Grace, to discover the meaning of death. It was all that mattered to her.

Our searches had been different based on what we sought to find. While I often sought comfort from my reading, much of Mary's reading, such as her reading on energy, was geared toward understanding the physical nature of life and death. What were we while we were here and what did we become when we left?

Mary only told us later about the underlying sense of urgency she had felt about going to the retreat, as if propelled to take this first step into uncharted territory. Propelled because she could take it with people she trusted.

Julie's approach to the retreat was almost clinical. She looked to it as she would a doctor's appointment at which she would hope to discover what was wrong and how to fix it.

Throughout the year, the three of us had been, for each other, almost a place of joining. Whatever happened, happened when we were away from each other and then was brought in, to the place of the three, for sharing, for examining, for understanding. Now, at the cabin, we would attempt to make something happen while we were together and it was new to us, foreign. We did not get together on weekends; we did not go to movies together. We had once or twice entertained each other in our homes. But this was different. It was like going to a church and not finding a priest or minister there. We did not know how to proceed. We were not totally at ease. We only knew that we had this precious, precious time and that we could not waste it.

We were so expectant, in fact, that we made ourselves anxious. Much like on one of our workdays of old (we had worked that day, leaving on a Thursday night), we arrived rushed and breathless: expectant. We had changed our milieu. We weren't in the office. We did not have tasks to structure our time around. We did not have familiarity. It seemed, at first, as if the retreat would be a bust. As if we would go home disappointed. We did not stay up talking all night. We were tired. Our expectations had drained us.

But the new day dawned differently. We had not wanted to waste time preparing food and so had just brought good bread and cheese and fruit. We ate a little and then we adjourned to the living room and sat on the floor with the sun coming through the windows. This was not a rustic cabin. The living room had floor-to-ceiling windows on two sides, floor-to-ceiling mirrors between wood beams on the other. The floor was carpeted in a plush, soft cream. Throw pillows abounded. A stereo played CDs we had brought: Van Morrison, Angela Bofill, U2, k.d. lang. We were sitting in the lap of luxury, surrounded by the green and gold of a dozen varieties of trees just beginning to wear their fall colors. They were right outside our windows and in the room as well— their reflection held in the mirrors—so that any way we turned, we were surrounded by nature and light.

As Mary was preparing to leave home to drive to the cabin, Amanda had given her a little gift she had made. It consisted of two popsicle sticks tied together with pink and white yarn to form a cross. When Amanda gave it to her she said, "Mom, take this with you. It's a God's Eye." Like at one of our workday morning updates, Mary brought out her God's Eye to show us. We sat on the floor, our bodies forming a little circle, and with the introduction of the God's Eye into the center of the circle, the circle became altarlike. When placed in the circle, the candles and incense I had brought to mask the smell of my cigarettes continued the theme. And when Mary brought forth the program from Grace's memorial service, it was very much as if we were in a holy place as she read the Litany of Memory:

At the rising of the sun and its going down
>We remember her

At the blowing of the wind and in the chill of
winter
>We remember her

At the opening of the buds and in the rebirth
of spring
>We remember her

At the blueness of the sky and in the warmth
of summer
>We remember her

At the rustling of leaves and in the beauty of
autumn
>We remember her

At the beginning of the year and when it ends
>We remember her

As long as we live, she too will live, for she is
now a part of us
>We remember her

We bowed our heads in silence.

Then it seemed as if the Litany of Memory and the objects we had brought were calling us to join hands and continue to pray. We asked our angels and Gracie to join us. We said words of prayer. Our hands did not feel natural linked with those of our friends. Our attempt to organize ourselves to action felt a bit stilted. But we

carried on, sitting on the floor, me in my robe and slippers, Mary in her sweat suit, all of us without our makeup, different to each other, but earnest and trying.

After our prayer, we were able to chat more easily,
more companionably than we had since we arrived. We
were sharing our dreams of the night before, each of
which had included glass in some way, when Mary jerked
and stared with an expression on her face akin to what
one might wear after having seen a mouse. Her gaze was
off to Julie's right and Julie jumped too, as if whatever it
was, was contagious. "What? What?" she cried, realizing
Mary had seen something—a spider maybe. Julie moved
a foot from where she had been sitting, casting her eyes
around for what it was Mary had seen.

Then Mary told us. "I saw light."

Mary described what she saw as a fairly large, conical
blue light that seemed to surround many smaller bubbles
of white light. It had been just to the right of Julie's shoul-
der. Mary was in awe. She said that while she gazed upon
it, she experienced the complete cessation of time.
Several days later I asked Peace about it and he said:

The light was Mary's own light and it was her Gracie as well.

Explain this to me, Peace.

*The blue light was Mary's own light projected out and filled by Grace.
Filled with Grace. You each have your own lights which are more truly
you than the bodily forms you are in. The truer you are being to the
self, the more visible the light becomes. The more you share and trust*

188

and connect, the more they expand to encompass those you share and trust and connect with. The clearest way I can describe it is that Mary's light reached out to Julie—not just at that instant, the room was charged with your lights—and that for a moment the light illuminated the presence of Mary's angel.

What do you mean by Mary's angel? Is Gracie Mary's angel?

Gracie will always be Mary's angel. This does not mean that she is also Mary's guide in all things. The term Guardian Angel *would fairly accurately describe what I am to you and what Trinity and Water are to Mary and Julie. But every being that has affected you in your life is, whether you feel the connection or not, connected to you. Those who have affected you and have passed out of this life to the next remain connected. Remember that when you called upon the angels, you called upon Gracie too. Do you think you could call upon her and not have her respond? This would be impossible. She was there and she was basking in her mother's light.*

Did she mean to become visible? And if so, why did she not become visible in a form Mary could recognize? And if not, was it an accident? Are accidents possible?

It is more an accident that you do not see than that you see. There is a little bit of each one of us in each other. When Mary sees herself, she will see Gracie—the essence of Gracie—as well. Maybe because Mary was not trying at that moment, her vision cleared and she saw in her light—in what might more accurately be called your combined lights—herself in love, and that is what Gracie is in her essence: light and love given form, light with substance, life subtly manifested.

189

Mary's seeing the light should have been enough for one day. Yet when we fell quiet, we once again felt awkward.

I had brought my computer at Julie's request, so that we could talk to Peace if we decided that was what we wanted to do. But it was as if none of us wanted to take charge and say let's do this or let's do that. We didn't quite know how to be but we knew to be respectful of one another. When we fell quiet, I went into the other room where I had set up my computer and opened the Peace file. I knew if the others wanted to join me they would.

Soon Julie came in and then left again to get Mary. Mary said she had been feeling "persnickety," resistant once again, and hadn't wanted to come. She was afraid Peace might say something bad about her. But Julie had said, "You've got to come now," and she came.

I addressed the angels, rather than Peace, and the first question I asked was if Mary's and Julie's angels were with us. Peace responded:

Their angels are where they are as I am where you are.

We're all feeling this energy so strongly. What does it mean?

It means you are connected. What once was one, singular, is now one, joined.

Julie: Thanks for joining us, for letting us feel you, for the release.

Julie is welcomed with open arms to our presence, our being, our reality. She can join us at any time. She can Remember now how to evoke what is within her all the time. She can Feel. She can fill with spirit. It is coming out from within. She is reflecting. You are a prism, Julie. You are your own rainbow to the divine, your own gateway. You only need to open like a flower opens to the sun—an unfolding. Unfold. Release. Let go. Let your light shine.

Julie's skin is like a conduit. With you, words are a conduit; with Julie, her very skin is—like an electrical field, attracting and repulsing depending on her openness or closedness. She will attract or repel what she desires in this way. Her most direct route to her goals is through opening and remaining open. Unfolding. As if there are layers and layers of swaddling wrapping her. Like an infant protected from the elements. Yet it is the elements she needs. She should stay away from all synthetics. She should not wear any unnatural fabrics against her skin for they block her connecting with the elements she needs to feel. She should be aware of the purifying nature of water. Ingesting water will help her to purify her body, her skin, her soul—for it is through her body, her skin, that she reaches her soul. Everyone is different in their access points. This is hers.

Look at her. It is in letting herself be seen that her unfolding will take place. People need to really look at her. To see her skin, her eyes, her hair, even her clothing. The reflection of being seen will show her herself.

For every need you let another fulfill, you fulfill a need. It is the exchange. And the exchange is very important for Julie. For everyone that sees her, she will grow. Every time she is seen, she will grow.

Julie: Meaning seen as in my true self—really letting my true nature be seen?

Yes! In being open to be seen, you remove the veils of illusion. You have been wrapped in the veils from head to toe. Your face is your visible point—your access point. Take off the mask and breathe.

Julie: But what if people don't like me? It's scary. It's scary to let these two know me.

Let go of the fear, sweet one. Open your heart. There is so much love waiting to flow in. You have no idea, you cannot comprehend the boundlessness of the love you have been blocking. When people see you, they will see love, pure love, divine love. You are worthy, unique, completely lovable in every way. When you let people see you, you will see this, because it will be reflected back to you. You may at first be stunned by it, by the strength of it. It is a powerhouse of love awaiting you.

    Befriend your fear for now. Pet it. Make a pet of it. A small thing. Something that can fit in a box or beneath a bed. It is small and will get smaller. Only in your mind is it huge. Think of what your daughter, Lucia, sees when she looks at you—of what Peter sees. Then think of giving this gift to the world. That is what you are—a gift to the world. You only need to unwrap yourself.

Mary: Hello to Peace and my Angel and to Gracie. I just want to thank you for coming into our lives. And I want you to know how grateful I am for Margaret's courage and Julie's light and how much it means to me. And I'm afraid to do this but you guys are helping me to do this.

You can ask, Mary. What is it you want to ask?

Mary: Am I just a big fear basket case?

You Know you are not. You Know so much more than you allow yourself to see. Is this fear blocking your path? Blocking you from knowing what you know? Yes. But you still Know. It is there, tappable when you are ready to tap into it. Like dipping a ladle in water. The well is deep. It will never run dry. It is a well of plenty, of abundance. Remember the abundance, drink from the well. Do not go thirsty. It is as if you have a tool—a dipper—and you choose to use a sieve. Choose the dipper. It is always your choice.

Mary: What will give me more clarity to see?

You already see. You Know this in the deepest part of yourself. Your clarity is like a pure, clear tone that you listen for—a whisper, a sigh. It is not the clarity of thunderstorms. It is the clarity of a gentle breeze. Your access is from the everyday, the beauty of the now. The way a curtain blows in through a window tells you more about the divine than many people know in a lifetime. And this is because you already Know. You only need to remember. And the daily reminders that you are beginning to recognize but sometimes think are not important are. They are!

Be gentle with yourself. You cannot be gentle enough. Treat yourself with loving care. It is in how you treat yourself that you will see how to treat others. There is a way in which you are your own guinea pig— your own testing ground. You find how to see self first and then you see the world. You learn how to comfort yourself first and then you comfort the world. The kindness you show yourself is paramount. Without this kindness to self, you cannot bring yourself to the world, and yourself, your Self is what the world needs from You. The world is incomplete without the trueness of you. You are like a link in a chain. Forget about being strong. It is in your weakness, your sweetness, your lovingness that your true strength is. You do not have to carry the burdens of the world on your shoulders. All the world asks from you is your love. Give yourself a break! A literal break! You are weighted down with the burdens you carry. Tell yourself that you deserve a break, a breather, a rest, a retreat. As often as you need. This is a key to the clarity you seek. Lay down your burdens and rest.

Mary: I don't know how very well. Can I get a little help?

Thank you, dear Mary, for asking. I will help you constantly. You do not even have to ask twice. I will show you the way. Let go of trying. You try so hard, dear one. Never has anyone tried so hard. It is as if you try hard even when there is nothing to do. You do not ever stop trying. I will help you remember. Now that you have asked, leave trying to me. I take it from you. You no longer need to try. If you never try again it will be too soon. Every time the word or the feeling of trying comes to you, tell yourself you gave that away. You no longer have trying in your vocabulary. Believe me.

Julie: Do children have a significance in the oneness?

They have a significance, a divine significance for you, Now, in this time, this space. Because you need them to learn to love yourself. When you have learned to love yourself, all people will be equally significant.

Julie: So does this mean you'll help me?

That's what it means. I heard you. You hear me.

Julie: Thanks. And I'll drink lots of water.

You are welcome and welcomed. Don't forget you are welcomed.

This is a condensed version of the afternoon, but even if it had been printed in its entirety, it could not capture the feelings, as I cannot capture the feelings. The closest I can come to describing what we all felt was a sense of being overwhelmed. Tears ran down our faces. I visibly shook as I typed the words. And there is no way in rereading the words to recapture the import that they had. There was wisdom in the words, but it was as if there was a wisdom outside of the words, a wisdom that could be felt, a wisdom that felt almost like a shared emotion.

My heart was beating so hard, I felt as if I had just run a race, as if I were flushed with it, and when I looked at Julie and Mary, their faces were flushed as well. Their hearts, too, they said, were racing, pumping, it seemed, with mine, beating the beat of oneness.

It was also the most peaceful I had ever felt about asking for messages for others. Perhaps because Julie and Mary were with me, feeling what I felt, interactive with the process, it wasn't so individually overwhelming. To be overwhelmed with the emotion when I was alone was completely different than when I was with Mary and Julie. Together we had a strength and a courage I did not have alone. Alone I felt an awesome responsibility; I experienced all those feelings of, *Who am I to be able to do this?* With them I felt only the miracle of it.

There was a peacefulness to it instead of an anxiety. I felt it immediately. And there was also a credibility. If any doubts lingered, they were now gone. We had not only received words, we had received feelings, and we had shared them. We had not only received words, but words that confirmed what we already knew: that we were connected. For Trinity had spoken almost the same words, about drinking from the well, to Mary once before, unbeknownst to me. And it seemed as if the words, given to her again through *my* fingers, were a gift that said, "Yes. You are connected. If you needed further proof, here it is."

And here it is—Trinity's words to Mary on June 17, 1995, which she did not share with me until December, when I began this book.

You are a well of love. Dip into the well and take a drink! Feel the coolness of the water, savor the taste of the water, let your body sing with this delight, this awakening. Put the ladle back. Lower the bucket. Know that the well is there for you always, with the cool, soothing, refreshing liquid of love.

Yet it wasn't only the words but also the tone of the words. Mary said that she could tell, feel, sense the change immediately when Trinity began to speak. She had been writing to Trinity for four months. She knew his voice. She *recognized* his voice. That I could access that voice, that my fingers could type Trinity's messages, was a miracle to her. It was the greatest sign any of us had had that we were connected by something beyond ourselves.

It was much later still before I realized the full impact of the messages. I had always seen or envisioned the mes-

196

sages as coming directly to me from the angels. Even though I was overwhelmed with emotion every time I had spoken to Peace or Water for Julie, I had not known where that emotion came from. I had remarked on it to Julie, to Mary. I was puzzled that I generally felt more emotion when I asked about Julie's concerns than when I asked about my own. It wasn't until the end of the year, when Mary asked Trinity a question for me, that the truth began to reveal itself. Because Trinity told Mary she was feeling my energy. And Mary knew that she was.

Even then I didn't see. I credited Mary's feeling my energy as a unique talent that she had, something produced by her awareness and interest in energy. But eventually I came to see, to know, that the overwhelming emotions I experienced when I asked for Julie were Julie's own overwhelming emotions.

This wasn't a lesson of this retreat, but it was a lesson so huge that not to mention it here would be to dilute the full measure of this story's message. Because the realization that another's feelings, energy, emotion, and spirit were accessible was a truly miraculous realization, more miraculous to me than that of being able to access a divine spirit. Because I had thought of divine spirits as different. Angels, after all, were not human, were not ordinary. Their function, if I could guess on it based on my limited experience, was to be message bearers.

I would have thought, before this realization came to me, that Julie's function was so entirely different, so entirely separate from my own, that communication of this sort between us would have been impossible. Nothing in what I had read had prepared me for this— not even the messages of other spirits such as Emmanuel or Orin. Yet I knew it was true and Julie, when I told her, knew too—in fact, had known at some inner level all along.

I was taken aback by this knowledge, newly amazed at Julie's courage, at her openness. If I had realized Mary would feel my energy when she spoke to Trinity for me, would I have asked it of her? This was the deepest possible knowing. And its implications went beyond anything I felt ready to deal with. It spoke to the very lessons we had been learning all along, but it changed everything. I thought I had realized our connectedness the previous spring. I hadn't.

Mary and Julie were more circumspect about this new dimension. And it was because they *had* realized the connectedness last spring. They knew they shared a bond, that they were connected in a way that I had no concept of until I realized I had felt Julie's emotional energy. I didn't understand how they could have dealt with this concept so easily, this concept that changed everything. But it hadn't necessarily been easy for them either. They had just been dealing with it longer than I. They had known almost from the beginning what I didn't learn until the end of the year. . . .

Those unseen connections we had talked about were

real! And they said something about the nature of the universe itself. They said something about the nature of us ordinary humans. They said just what I had said here, earlier, thinking I understood it when I didn't understand it at all: that we are not meant to be separate and alone. Are not meant to be alone and lonely. For we must be joined. If I am to believe my own experience, I must believe, too, that we are not as ordinary as I once had thought. That something links us. Something that makes us accessible to one another.

XIX

SAFETY

As I left work a few days after the retreat, still trying
to define the new feeling of peacefulness that had
come over me, the word *safe* came to mind. I realized "safe" was how I had felt since the cabin. The next
day I went into work and told Julie how I had defined
what I was feeling as safe, and she got that "this is unbe-
lievable" look on her face, and she said safe was exactly
how she had felt. Finally, Mary came back to work after
having been out sick for two days, happy, glowing, warm,

so excited to talk to us she was ready to bust. She had gotten safety out of the weekend too, and she had never expected to feel safe again after her daughter's death.

The power of what had happened at the cabin stayed with us. And it led me to take a class that began in late September, a class titled "Ways of Knowing."

When I saw the title of the class in the university bulletin, it seemed as if it was meant for me. I had discovered, through Julie, the *Noetic Sciences Review,* a journal that explores our "ways of knowing," even before I discovered its president, Willis Harman. And through the journal I had found more readings to accompany me on my journey. Here was science, once again, exploring the same ideas that I was exploring in the context of spirituality. A science that seemed open to the limitless possibilities of the human mind, the human subconscious.

One of the reasons I decided to take the class was my new feeling of being safe in the world. And it seemed that the place of safety was as good a place as any from which to rejoin that world. The inward journey had been going on for nine months: the length of a pregnancy. It seemed time to give birth to this new self I had been becoming. To bring it into the world and see what it would find there and what it would be.

I was not alone in either my feeling of safety or my desire to take advantage of it. We had all found it during our spirit sister retreat and we all found it a luxury we could not afford to waste. At times it felt as if it were a

201

new car or a shiny new sailboat or some space-age vehicle that would know the most expeditious route to where we were going. At other times, it felt like a place from which we could launch ourselves, a place of sure-footing, an even ground from which we could get a running start. It was like being handed a break, like an athlete being seen by a scout. It was a window of opportunity, transparent with possibility. It seemed to call us to venture into the world again.

While in reality we had never left the real world of ordinary life, the feeling of safety seemed to contradict this notion of reality. It seemed to say we had. That we had been somewhere else. We had visited a foreign land and now we were home safe. Safe. We had been in retreat all along and now it was time to forge ahead. It seemed to say we were *ready!* It seemed to say *begin!*

We had a new and different energy level that we yearned to expend on what was important. Work became something to get done in a hurry so that we could go on to other things. And amazingly, it did get done in a hurry. We became extremely efficient. We started talking about completing tasks in terms of minutes rather than days and hours. "Oh, I can have that mailing, that memo, that budget done in seven minutes." Sometimes it was a joke. Sometimes it wasn't. Mary began to have dreams in which I was always on vacation and she was always getting twice as much work done at superhuman speed. I began to have retreat dreams. Over and over, dreams of

202

being at a lodge or cabin with women friends surrounding me, with time and space to *be* surrounding me.

The only problem was that we still weren't sure what, besides the spiritual journey, was important. I was stymied in my writing because I could not tear myself away from the Peace writing long enough to pursue new projects or decide what to do about either the old or the new. So I chose a class. Mary, while trying for a new baby, was looking for ways to turn the ordinary into the beautiful. Julie was on her way to realizing music played some part in her destiny. We all wanted to begin. We could not begin fast enough. But what were we to do?

The quest had subtly changed from one of "Who am I?" to one of "What am I to do with who I am?" The feelings of it were just as primal, just as spiritual. Julie was no longer content to receive a paycheck for a job. She sought a calling!

What was our purpose? What did God have in mind for us? What was our contribution to be? What unique talents did we possess that the world was waiting for? Although the angels seemed to have been telling us that the world was simply waiting for us, the real us, to emerge, we added a spin in one part unique to our culture and our time, in one part universal. This place of safety seemed to call us to not just be, but to be all we could be, the best we could be. It seemed to say, jump in, the water is fine.

I bring up my class again because it was largely a class on philosophy. It looked at the great thinkers of the past and how they determined how we know what we know. Then it looked at present-day thinkers, many of them women, many of them women of color. People who came at our ways of knowing from a completely different place than men of old. It excited me. I inwardly applied all the arguments to spirituality and felt that I kept validating what I knew. It was invigorating. Until I wrote a paper discussing how our ways of knowing are different when we approach them from a place of safety. Until I realized the professor had no idea what I was talking about.

My vocabulary had changed. It was different. The same words had new meaning. This had been happening to Mary, Julie, and me all along, but I had not realized how complete the transformation was until that moment. I realized no one in academia would understand what I knew unless I talked about God. Unless they understood the new meanings everything had. This discouraged me from the class, but it added a new dimension to my reality. I had changed. My world had changed. My *words* had changed. And the only ones who understood the change were my spirit sisters.

Mary perhaps came closest to describing safety when she called it a "way of being." We did not realize we had not felt safe before because we had not realized how safety felt. None of us had ever experienced it, either within ourselves or with anyone else. It was like realizing that we had spent our whole lives waiting for the next bad thing to happen and that this hadn't been a passive waiting. We had waited with anxiety, with the feeling of lurking danger or disaster. Our lives had been, until this point, about trying to keep the next bad thing from happening, trying to stay one step ahead of the game, trying to be prepared for the worst.

But for Mary, when Grace died, the worst had literally happened. And, as much as anyone other than her family could, Julie and I had been through the worst with her.

And now here we were, feeling safe. What had happened?

Waiting for the next bad thing—for the worst to happen—had felt normal before. What we had learned through Grace's life and death was that this was not normal. Now we could see it for what it was: fear. We had all been living in fear. Fear was what we had called normal.

Safety was the absence of fear. Safety was, according to the dictionary, freedom from danger, injury, or damage.

We might not have literally spent every day of our lives feeling as if we were in mortal danger, but we had spent our lives feeling that we were at the mercy of life, at the whim of fate. Fearing that for all our hard work, despite whatever minimal control we could exert, what we had to look forward to was simply the luck of the draw, was life having mercy on us. Life refraining, if we were lucky, from harming or punishing us, its offenders, its enemies, we who were in its power.

The words we used, either for or against ourselves, whether conscious or subconscious, made up our thoughts. Where our words, and thus our thoughts, had previously been full of the danger and fear, the punishment and doom we had been expecting, they now reflected our new feelings. This place of safety seemed to say that if we weren't in control, it wasn't fate or luck that was, but God.

Taking the class showed me that others did not know they were living in fear any more than Mary and Julie and I had before our retreat. This is why they could not understand safety as we understood it: because they did not understand fear. We learned that what we knew and how we knew it were different now that we were not looking at the world through fearful eyes.

The Ways of Knowing class had been about what and whom we trusted. Did we come to feel we knew what we knew by listening to what experts thought? by listening to the media? by studying history and philosophy? What proof did we need to convince us of new knowledge? Whom did we trust? Who was the final authority? Everything was suspect. Especially us. Especially our own ways of knowing. No one even asked if we trusted ourselves. It was as if everything that was knowable was outside of ourselves.

The experiences of our year had taught us to know things on a new level. To know from within, based on our own internal authority rather than any external authority. What we had learned together had given us more than any class we had ever taken—more than the combined knowledge we had acquired from years of schooling. It was our first inkling that knowing ourselves was what it was all about.

And, as if to prove that now that we were safe we were also ready, real life intervened and pushed us from the nest. We had literal journeys to embark upon in October. Mary and I would go to New Orleans, Julie to San Francisco. We would return and all of us would depart for Europe. It was that time of year on the calendar. It was work once again. Work that couldn't be compressed into seven minutes. It was life and we looked forward to it. A literal journey to correspond with our inward journeys. To bring us back into the world.

XX

CONTEMPLATION

Before our spirit sister retreat, I had discovered the word *contemplation*. In James Hillman's *Insearch: Psychology and Religion,* I read: "Curiosity about fact and detail gives way before the open contemplation of what is, just as it comes."[4]

We had gone to the retreat with contemplation. We went forward on our worldly journeys with a state of contemplation as well, a state not active but open. We were together for a part of our journeys, apart for a

CONTEMPLATION

longer period. What we each contemplated was totally different. How we each reacted was totally different. But the result was the same.

The part of our literal journeys when the three of us would be together would be spent in Barcelona. Two firsts were occurring. We had never before had our jobs offer us the opportunity to travel as a threesome, and we had never before had the chance to travel overseas. We did not go alone, however. My mother and I had long planned a trip to Italy to visit relatives. Being in Barcelona for work afforded me the opportunity to make the trip to Italy more cost effectively and I asked her to join me. From there sprang the idea of also having Mary's mother accompany us. The two mothers could keep each other company while we worked. And finally, Julie brought her husband, Kelly.

We had talked excitedly for months of the possibilities that awaited us. Because we were contemplating something new, something none of us had done before, we had no expectations except those of pleasure. We would be together. We would be in life and away from our ordinary lives. Anything could happen. And it did.

We had barely entered the lobby of our hotel when the unexpected occurred. Julie, catching up with a woman attending the symposium we were putting on, brought out her pictures of her new baby, the now one-year-old Peter. And Mary plummeted. She had no pictures to share.

Pictures had been shared before. Peter had visited the

209

office. Mary had felt no pain. Mary looked at Peter and imagined how Grace would be. He was a visual representation of how Grace would have been had she lived. Mary looked on him with awe and wonder. She rejoiced in the love that visibly linked Peter and his mother, knowing that the same love linked her and Grace in a different way.

But now she mourned anew. Now the pictures were a reminder that Grace wasn't with her. There was no explaining why the pain had waited, why the pictures shared in a lobby in Barcelona more than a year after Grace's death had triggered a fresh bout of mourning. But there was also no denying it.

Mary did not want her pain to affect us. She isolated herself. When she wasn't working, she was in bed. Crying. She fought with her mother. We each wondered what had caused Mary's mood. We each asked, "Is something wrong?" But this time Mary could not share her feelings. She could not say, "Julie shared her pictures of Peter and I had none to share." So she said nothing.

Mary grew angry and sought to understand her anger. She grew sad and sought to understand her sadness. She was on vacation, she "should" have been enjoying herself. But the sadness had waited. The anger had waited. They had waited for her to be open to them; then they waited for her to identify them before she could go on.

Julie's experience was similar.

Julie traveled on from Barcelona with her husband on

what should have been a second honeymoon, a time of relaxation and joy. But she could not relax, could not enjoy. She found she did not know how to *be* without her children, without the mother and worker roles she played in her everyday life. She was not happy and she was mad that she was not happy.

For me, having expected to share the pleasure of the journey with my two friends, their discomfort was a source of perplexity and insecurity. What was wrong? Why weren't they sharing what was wrong? In order to enjoy my vacation, I had to let Mary's feelings be Mary's feelings, Julie's be hers. I had to accept that I could not fix things—that some things just had to be allowed to be what they were. I went on from Barcelona with this thought in my mind. I went on seeking added meaning for my spiritual quest. I found it.

How could anyone be luckier than to go to Rome, to Assisi and Florence and Milan in the middle of a spiritual quest? I could not fail to see that the glory of God and the glory of humanity were reflective of one another. I could not fail to see that the "faithful" who flocked to holy places were seekers, just as Julie, Mary, and I were. I felt a connection to God and to the whole.

What we each contemplated was totally different. How we each reacted was totally different. But the result was the same: gratitude.

XXI

GRATITUDE

Appropriately, it was in November, at the time of Thanksgiving, when we reached a place of gratitude. We had gone out into the world and had returned grateful. Each in our own way.

Mary, who had returned from the trip first, found her gratefulness first.

She had finally allowed herself to feel her sadness, to embrace her anger. In all the time since her daughter's death, throughout all we had shared, Mary had withheld her anger, had withheld that deep, wrenching, heart-breaking sadness of grief. She had withheld it from us because she had been holding it all within. Now she had felt it and released it. Now she had allowed herself to move through it and to reach the other side. Having done so allowed her to feel closer to herself, to know all the sides of her humanness and make them one. She had felt the emptiness of what she didn't have and moved past it to gratitude for what she did have.

Julie, the next to return, returned determined. Her photographs of her trip told the whole story. There she was, a person unable to enjoy herself. Now she was home and she was going to be different. She was determined. She was going to enjoy what she had.

I waited two days after I returned from Europe to call anyone. I waited because I did not want anything to disturb me. I had at last found joy! And it was, as Peace had been telling me, right in front of me. It was what I had. It was my ordinary life, my present. It was found in appreciation for what I had just as soon as I quit longing for what I didn't have.

When I began to call people, I would tell them, "These past few days have been the happiest of my life." People expected to hear about Europe. I could hardly quit talking about home.

I knew my contentment with the present, that my joy, was fragile. Part of it centered on my foresight at planning my vacation so that it extended through Thanksgiving week. I could be a hermit for a few days. I could live within my own personal heaven. I could wipe my counters, polish my furniture, hold my husband, kiss my children, putter around my house, listen to my music, look out the window at my yard, the same trees, the same birds, the new beauty of it all.

We were going to host Thanksgiving for my husband's family. Our first holiday in our new home. Yet I did not think about it, in those first days.

Christmas was approaching. I generally had my shopping done by this time. Yet I did not think about it, in those first days.

I avoided the newspaper, especially the advertisements. I avoided television. I avoided thinking about paying my post-trip bills. I just *was* for a few glorious days.

Then I phoned the office. I told Mary, as I had told everyone else, that I was happy, grateful, so appreciative of my home and family. She told me she and Julie had felt the same way on their return. All the spirit sisters were grateful!

When I talked to Mary on the phone, I could tell that whatever place she had been at in Barcelona no longer existed. She had not needed to tell me she was happy. I could hear it in her voice as clearly as, I'm sure, she could hear my happiness in mine.

And I could feel the difference the instant I saw Mary and Julie again when I went back to work after Thanksgiving. I knew that our relationships had proceeded to a higher level, that everything was good between us. I knew it was not just me. We had, at least with each other, transcended our ordinary shortcomings. No pettiness remained. No barriers. We were grateful for each other.

I hadn't often remembered, during my travels, my night-time prayer: "I am not separate; I can trust; I can know; I am responsible; I am single-minded. My greatest desire is to know the desire of my higher will." But now it came to mind and made me realize what was different.

That final line was what it had all been about for each of us in the past few months. *Knowing.* And I came to see that what was new was our understanding that knowing would come when the time was right. Accepting that we would know. Somehow, our return from our travels had ushered in a time of finding the value of patience, of stillness, of waiting, and of doing it with gratitude rather than resentment. We hoped our wanting to know was a desire that sprang from contemplation, a desire to serve. And we realized that, perhaps for now, it was service to ourselves and our families that was required.

We weren't any more sure of anything than we had ever been. We were still just ordinary women. But we accepted that we did not know what was to be and did not have to know.

What we each had found was that gratitude was not possible without a prerequisite. That prerequisite was acceptance.

We became safe. We went out into the world. And we

returned, first, foremost, and finally, accepting. We were so grateful, we leapt right over the act of acceptance to enjoy our gratitude. We almost missed it.

But could Mary ever really feel gratitude without accepting the death of Grace? Could Julie ever really feel gratitude without accepting where she was at the present time and how she had come to be there? Could I feel gratitude while I continued to believe my happiness rested on an external such as being a published writer?

Acceptance. And through acceptance of what *was* we were released from the final barriers to our connectedness. The envy, competition, distrust, hurt feelings that had come and gone throughout our year together were to be no more.

We had finally accepted ourselves—as we were—all of ourselves. We no longer said I accept this but I don't accept that. We would still wonder, we would still question, but we would find that wondering and questioning did not shake our acceptance. We accepted ourselves. And from the acceptance of our *selves,* we finally, completely, totally, accepted one another.

XXII

GIVING

As Christmas approached, we each tried to turn our backs on commercialism, to do Christmas right, and to find ways to be moved by the real message of Christmas. And surprisingly, we each found it for ourselves by beginning to understand the phrase "give and you shall receive."

I had always thought the saying was a little odd—as if the purpose of giving was to receive something in return. But it was not about that at all. What it meant was give and you will receive *through* your giving. My spirit sisters and I had been learning this lesson all along. The biggest lessons were yet to come.

Giving, like sharing, like suspending judgment, had two sides to it.

The first began with giving as we commonly know it. The giving of a gift, a bit of advice, compassion, humor, knowledge. We thought this kind of giving was what our year had been about. Until we saw that our giving had gone beyond this giving as we commonly knew it. The Christmas season showed us how much we received *through* our giving. That true giving was circular in motion.

With one another we were teachers and learners equally. By being so we realized we never lost one thing by giving. That we *had to* give in order to receive. That the more we gave the more we got. The more we gave the more we grew. That in being open to one another as teachers, as learners, we had given of ourselves. Not parts of ourselves. All of ourselves. Because we were no longer divided, because we no longer saw one part of ourselves as good enough to give and another part as unworthy of giving, we truly gave for the first time in our lives and just as truly received.

It was no accident, no coincidence that we had learned each lesson of the year together, simultaneously, that we were in sync. It couldn't be any other way because what we gave we received and what we received we gave. Circular.

We didn't *make* confessions to one another. We *gave* them. And how we benefited through our giving! We rid ourselves of painful burdens we had carried at the same time that we gave a gift that said, I trust you, I want to be *who I am* with you. By *giving* our confessions, we *could* be who we were. We saw that what we had so long held on to in fear and in pain, *could* be given up. That all the energy we had used to suppress what we thought we could not reveal could be freed. That we could reclaim the power we had given those things over us. From the simple act of *giving* our confessions, so much was received in return! From giving confessions, we learned to *give* forgiveness—a giving that, in true circular fashion, returned to us so that we could eventually give forgiveness to ourselves.

We didn't come to know hope and sharing and connectedness through some form of osmosis. We came to know through the act of giving and through the act of receiving. And we found that the gifts we gave kept *on* giving. They stayed with us. Once we began to forgive ourselves, that forgiveness reached into our pasts to forgive all of ourselves, reached into our pasts to forgive others, and came into the present to forgive as we went along. The suspension of judgment, too, was a gift—a gift for life. We would never be done with it, anymore than we would be done with forgiveness. What we gave and what we received, like what we learned, would be forever.

But there was another side to giving that was equally important. The other side of giving was *giving up.*

Trinity had asked Mary to give up trying. To give it to him. Peace often asked me to give things away, things like guilt and worry. Water had urged Julie to make a pet of her fear until the time came when she could give it up for good.

It was about *giving up* control. We didn't have it anyway. But while we thought we did, we struggled. It was about laying down our burdens so that we could quit struggling and rest. So that we could get closer to that still, quiet voice within.

It was another way of saying let go. Let go of those things that did us no good—like judgment and guilt. We just hadn't yet learned that it also applied to our greatest desires and fears.

XXIII

ANSWERS

The end of our year began to reveal itself as being about confronting our greatest desires and our greatest fears. We were all seeing that our jobs were no longer enough, could no longer be our goal and our mission. Our purpose. And we were each seeing that this left a void. Something had to take its place. We turned to our greatest desires to fill the space of goal and mission our jobs no longer filled. We turned to our greatest desires to give us our purpose. The first lesson we learned was that our greatest desires *were* our greatest fears.

Mine was writing. Mary's was mothering. Julie's was expressing herself.

They were all about producing something to fill the void. Something to fill our lives, to give them meaning, to take up our time, to enable us to make a contribution. They were all about externals.

Being asked to confront our greatest desires, our greatest fears, showed us what power they had over us. They had power because we gave it to them. We gave these things the premier position of being our *answers.* Being a published writer was the *answer* for me. Being a mother the *answer* for Mary. Finding a means of expression the *answer* for Julie.

No matter how different our greatest desires and fears were, they were all, in the end, about the same thing— they were about having an answer, a solution to the problem of not seeing where we were as good enough.

As much as we were shaped by our culture, influenced by the best-seller list and other trends, we were also part of a culture in which we had begun to refer to ourselves as things such as consumers and products. We had started to believe that it was our culture, our education, our families that had produced what we were, and if we were not producing in turn, we were doing nothing, were nothing.

So integral was this belief to our culture, to our nation, to our very way of life, that we did not see it as being as insidious as it was. Mary wrote in her journal about her need to produce; about how a good day was a day during which she had been productive. Julie lamented over being unable to produce all she desired because of her young children. When my greatest desire/greatest fear took me over, it no longer mattered to me that I loved to write if the pages I wrote weren't in a form I could turn into a product.

We had not yet separated our thinking from that of a culture that valued producing and consuming above all else. We were, in fact, so entrenched in it that even in the midst of the transforming events of our year, we *stopped* in order to discover what to *do*—in order to be productive.

We had been seeking purpose. Where was it? Somewhere beyond our grasp, outside of the office, outside of the three?

We were all mothers. We were all educated and saw the way our children were educated. Education, like so much else in our culture, was about production. How many worksheets on math, spelling, history did our children do in a week? Our children's productions became their grades, became their success or lack thereof, became who they were. Our jobs were about producing. Education for adults was about getting jobs or keeping them: being productive. The goals were all "out there" somewhere. Waiting. Even education had become about production instead of about understanding. And production was becoming increasingly about information.

It was as if we were being told that when we collected

enough information, we would know what to do. Information was the "in" thing and the wave of the future. It was all there waiting on the Internet, the World Wide Web, the information highway. That call to connect electronically. To see ourselves as machines, the brain being the computer control center. And to see things as animate; the computer with its brain, as susceptible to viruses as the human body.

So it was that I didn't see right away that I had begun to expect the angelic messages to be another source of information. I didn't see that my questing had become one of looking for facts as I would look for an answer in an encyclopedia. My seeking for one answer had blinded me to everything except what I sought to find.

My spirit sisters knew of my desires, as I knew of theirs, and had similarly looked for answers from the angels. Julie had asked more than once for me to talk to Peace about her purpose. His answer invariably had been for her to seek within for her answer, even while offering clues that were tantalizing. Mary had asked if she would have another baby. Her answers seemed to suggest that she would but still she waited.

When our greatest desires/greatest fears took us over, we could not *see* that no answer would be good enough, we were simply driven to seek an answer. Since I had asked about my writing dilemma so many times from Peace without satisfaction, I even turned to Mary. If I couldn't get the information I sought out of Peace, maybe she could get it out of Trinity. I asked her to ask Trinity for advice on my writing. Why was I stuck? In which direction should I go? Mary asked and Trinity answered:

Her writing will unfold as a flower does. You will see. Will be there.

Go to your dreams. You SEE. You know. Margaret looks too hard at what already is in front of her—around her, within her. Look to your dreams. This is not difficult. It unfolds, as a flower does.

Patience is a friend during this time—especially for Margaret. It is there. Trust. BELIEVE.

This trust is paramount. As you see you share, all of you do, this unfolds. The story unfolds. You trust, you share, you grow. This is life. This is what dreams are made of. This is LOVE.

I thanked Mary and Trinity for this response, but because I was looking for *my* answer, an answer I believed I already knew even while I sought for it, I did not *see* Trinity's response for the answer that it was.

I continued my reading, continued my searching, all with an eye to supporting my goal, to defining and clarifying my answer. What I didn't realize, what Mary and Julie didn't realize, was that we had to separate production from purpose or we would never be happier than we were, more content than we were, be more than we were. We would always be seeking. We would never realize what we had found.

XXIV

TRUST

We knew we had been caught up in extraordinary events. We knew these events had been improving our lives. We knew we were kinder, more peaceful, more loving, more accepting. Life felt easier, gentler, more meaningful. But we thought that without an external purpose, something was incomplete, that *we* were incomplete.

Even while we sought what we thought would make us complete, a part of each of us tried not to pin our hopes on those things—because those things might not come to be. I might not ever be published. Mary might not ever conceive. Julie might not ever discover her calling. We tried to be content with where we were and what we had, we *were* more content than we had ever been, and yet our very belief in a more loving God, a more loving universe, made us, at the same time, more hopeful than ever before. It seemed as if we were caught in a double bind: we knew we should be accepting and happy in our present lives, but how did we reconcile present happiness with future longing? If God made us who we were, didn't our desires also come from Him?

We each now had an expectation of happiness. Fulfillment seemed to be a promise that was held out by this new life we had begun to experience. We simply could no longer believe that our ordinary lives and our work at the university were all that were available to us.

We knew there was more to life than what we had earlier expected and had been willing to accept. Where a year previously I had been willing to accept the notion of eventually retiring from the university, this no longer seemed an adequate use of the life God had given me. While Julie had been previously content to make a living, now she expected that she had something unique to offer and that she would not be fulfilled until she could discover what that was and accomplish it. Mary thought the least of her future work life because it seemed her life would go unfulfilled if she could not give the love and nurturing she had found within herself to another child.

Despite the events of our transformative year, we were still living our lives as if what happened in them was up to us. Still living our lives as if we knew what would make us truly happy. Still living as if . . . if we but wished for it, willed it, planned for it . . . we could make it be.

We were still living our lives as if we knew what our answers were.

This is where all the lessons of the previous year had to come together. This is where we had to integrate what we had learned into our lives. The feelings we had experienced earlier concerning going out into the world while still preparing had been accurate. We hadn't been ready yet, because we hadn't put it all together yet. As much as we thought we had been listening, as much as we thought we had been hearing, when it came to our greatest desires/greatest fears, what we had really been doing was saying, "Thanks very much for your answer. Now what about my answer?"

We had recognized a force greater than ourselves at work in the universe, but we hadn't fully realized the impact of that force upon our lives. The totality of our connection to it. Its link with us. Its power.

We hadn't really recognized God. We hadn't yet invited Him in.

For before this point, the learning really had been about ourselves. About our humanness, about living the day-to-day ordinary life.

Now the learning was about something greater than ourselves. About our divinity rather than our humanity, about living the day-to-day life in an extraordinary rather than an ordinary way. While we continued to think in ordinary terms, we would limit ourselves to the ordinary.

While I continued to think finding a publisher for my mystery novel would be the ultimate achievement of my life, while Julie continued to think finding her calling was hers, while Mary continued to think having a baby was hers, we were limiting ourselves. We could see it when we looked at each other. Mary and I could see that Julie would never *be* her career, no matter how fulfilling she found it; Mary and Julie could see that one book or twenty on the bookshelves would not define my life; Julie and I could see that Mary would always be more than a mother whether she had another child or not.

Now was the time for letting go of our ordinary ideas about ourselves. Now was the time for seeing that if we could truly suspend our judgment, Someone else would judge for us and judge us good and innocent; if we could really forgive ourselves, we could be worthy of what He might offer us; if we could really surrender, we could rest.

If we could trust, Someone else who really knew what would make us happy would plan for us.

It wouldn't be up to us anymore. It had never been up to us anyway.

On the day we began our spiritual retreat, I had purchased

the book *A Course in Miracles* and had been reading it daily ever since. On December 18, after failing to find the answer to my greatest desire/greatest fear, after failing to come to peace with my writing, I felt hopeless for the first time. Everything in my life was better. Everything except this. My greatest desire/greatest fear, like the desires and fears of Mary and Julie, had produced nothing but conflict. It seemed that these desires and fears were the only things that could still lead any of us out of peace. We would be moving along just fine and then these desires, these fears, would trip us up. We would become frustrated with not being able to force what we wanted out of our lives. Like a revolving door, we would start with the Why questions again: Why couldn't I publish? Why couldn't Mary conceive? Why didn't Julie know what she wanted to do?

It was something we were all beginning to see clearly but that we were unsure what to do about.

My hopelessness of December 18 led me to pick up *A Course in Miracles* and find within it a passage that told me I could give all of my decisions to the Holy Spirit. That He would solve any problem in the way that was best for everyone that would be affected by it. And in my hopelessness, I said take this from me. I don't want to be conflicted about it anymore. You decide if I should write or not, or if I should write, what I should write. I had realized that if I could not have peace *and* writing, it was the writing I would give up.

What I did that night was give up the illusion that I was

in control of my life. It was totally different than giving up guilt or judgment. Without realizing it, the lessons of the year had finally come together in my mind and heart.

XXV

PURPOSE

On December 19, 1995, I knew this book would be written. The decision was made at my kitchen table over a conversation with my friend Mary Love.

It was a day on which I was going to go Christmas shopping. I had written a list, even though I had been trying to give up making lists in favor of doing. Angela, who had just gotten her driver's license and just as quickly lost her head over the ensuing freedom, was consequently taking the bus that morning. I didn't have to drive her to school. This was the first break in my routine.

I also wasn't scheduled to work; I had taken vacation for the week, and before the shopping day began, I was going to roll out cookie dough that I'd prepared the day before and left chilling in the refrigerator. I didn't know if it was because of these things I had planned to do or if it was for other reasons that I felt anxious, but I did. And I'd come to a place already, by this time, where I expected to be able to control anxiety or at least to determine where the anxiety was coming from.

Because of this anxiety, I sat down to a bowl of cereal and a book. It was before eight and I told myself that at eight I would get up and go about my business. But the anxiety persisted, along with a desire to talk to Mary. I realized, eventually, that I was biding my time, waiting for her to arrive at work so that I could call her. Just as quickly, I realized that if I invited her, she might join me for coffee before she went to work. I phoned her and she said she'd come.

I was still in my robe and the pajama top in which I had slept. I didn't feel a need to dress but I slipped on my pajama bottoms, made a fresh pot of coffee, did up the breakfast dishes, and put Christmas cookies on the table. When Mary still hadn't arrived, I decided I had time to set a mood and put on classical Christmas music and lit some incense. Appropriately, it began to snow. The morning was just growing light and the Christmas tree sparkled in

233

front of my large living room window as Mary came in the door.

As soon as Mary came to my table, I knew why she had come, why I had felt anxious. I needed to tell her of my decision of the night before, of the place I had reached, both with my spiritual quest and my desire and fear of writing. Because what had felt like frustration the night before, in the morning light felt bigger than that. I knew some shift had occurred but I didn't know what it was.

Mary did. Mary not only understood, but said she had awakened to a message for me. That message was, *This is the story.*

Mary said she knew that what was meant by "the story" was *our* story, what was happening to us, the story of the spirit sisters, the story of what could happen to three ordinary women. As if to emphasize the rightness and certainty of the message, Mary's voice took on an otherworldly presence, an echo, a power. *This is the story.* There was no uncertainty. Nothing like it had ever happened to either of us before.

And I realized, right then, right there, that Mary was giving me my answer from the Holy Spirit. I had asked him to make my decision and He sent me an answer the very next morning. He sent me Mary and she knew what I was to *do.*

She, like me, was afraid to have what she *knew* taken for knowledge, taken for *the answer.* She worried, *What if it just came from me?* But I wasn't the only one who knew. Sitting in the morning light at my kitchen table, warming our hands on round little blue coffee cups, we could not deny that we knew. Because we could not deny that a new place had been reached within us. A place of trust. A place not of trusting in *our* answers, but of trusting in God's answer.

On December 19, the writing that had long been my goal was given to me like a gift. Another giving that I received in friendship, as an act of friendship. I thought it was the ultimate gift, given because I had reached the ultimate place, the place of trust. It felt like the ultimate gift because I had asked and had been answered. I felt as if for the first time in my life I knew exactly what to do, I was certain about something, there was no doubt in me. If this was what it was like to have a relationship with God, I knew there was nothing better.

But feeling as if we had reached a place that couldn't get any better was familiar by now. It was a feeling we had experienced before at other places along the path. My spirit sisters and I had thought finding hope was the greatest place until we found "suspend judgment," and that the suspension of judgment was the greatest thing going until we surrendered, and that surrender was the ultimate feeling until we arrived at safety, and gratitude the very best of places to be until we found trust.

As great as I felt to have my answer, that answer still had only been one of knowing what to do. Perhaps part of the reason that I was given such a clear answer was so that we would all learn to separate production from purpose. We all might have a unique contribution to make, a divine "something" to do in our lives, but what we do is still not what we are. The product we would produce, while it might become our goal for a little while, could not sustain us.

We each needed to realize that seeking purpose outside of ourselves was not what it was all about. Seeing our purposes as producing something outside of ourselves was just another error in judgment.

Purpose is innate. Something everyone has. Universal. As unseen as love. It wasn't "out there." It was inside. It wasn't about producing. It was about being.

Purpose doesn't change. Purpose has to go deeper than goals to find stability. Goals change. They aren't always meaningful. They are sometimes accidental. They often involve settling for less—settling for something achievable, producible.

What we came to find was that purpose is, by design, as much a part of us as our vital organs, as our spirit and soul. Something God gave us. Something we were born with.

It was something little Grace had.

It was something three ordinary women found for a while and almost didn't see as they searched for something else.

Purpose is something you cannot lose, so it cannot be a job or money or even a calling or a dream. Purpose is something that cannot fail, so it cannot be a goal one wishes to achieve but may not. Purpose is something that cannot be taken away, so it cannot be another person, or a home, or even the respect of others.

Purpose has to be inside the heart, the soul, the spirit. Because purpose is about *who we are* and how we choose to live—in whatever circumstance. It is about the intentional effect our lives have on others—as little Grace's life affected each of ours. It is about living our lives as God intended them to be lived rather than as we have determined they should be. Purpose is about God's intention, not ours.

To learn the final lesson of purpose, my goal of writing had to be shared with the spirit sisters. It had to be shared so that we would realize we shared a common purpose.

XXVI

LOVE

I t was in collaborating on the writing of *Love* that we
learned together that the end and the goal and the
purpose was the love itself.

Writing this story was an act of friendship and of love.
It wasn't about me and my goal—me in the singular, my
goal in the singular. It was bigger than that. It seemed for
a while that it was about us. About our learning, our
sharing, our combined purpose. Learning that it was bigger than all of us was the final lesson.

As we worked to create *Love* out of the story of three ordinary women, we realized that the attainment of our individual goals could not be the end, the reward, the purpose of our journeys or our lives. Our individual goals—our wanting of only one thing for only one person—as much as we might have thought of them as the most important things to us, were, finally, only goals. And goals were, finally, limits.

There is another error in our judgment much more difficult to see than that of self-criticism. It is the thinking that says that by setting a goal and achieving that goal, all is attained. When the error of this limited thinking was corrected, we saw that limiting ourselves was impossible once a combined purpose—a higher purpose—was realized.

We had needed to see and contemplate the whole story, see it in black and white—in the written form—before we could *see* with fresh eyes, the real message we had been given about purpose:

As you see you share, all of you do, this unfolds. The story unfolds. You trust, you share, you grow. This is life. This is what dreams are made of. This is LOVE.

When Trinity and Mary and the Holy Spirit, and later Peace told me my purpose was about *Love*, they were clearly telling me to write the story, to produce the story, but I was as clearly told I could not do it alone. It had to unfold from the love and the trust and the sharing of *all of us.*

When I was told my purpose was *Love,* it was the love itself that was being spoken of—not the book. It was about the effect the messages of *Love* would have in the world—not the product. It was about the love Mary, Julie, and I shared—not just the story.

Our search for one answer, our quest for information, our desire to produce was what had kept us from seeing. Looking at our goals separately from those of each other, separately from those of the whole, was what had kept us from recognizing the connecting force that had been at work throughout the story, throughout our year. The force that connected us to each other and to the whole. That connecting force was love.

I couldn't believe, when months later I reread Trinity's message, that I had ever missed it. Trinity was right that the story was about love, and Trinity was right when he said, "Margaret looks too hard at what already is in front of her—around her, within her." I looked so hard that I didn't *see* what *was.*

I was so blown away when I reread and finally *saw* Trinity's message, that I immediately called Mary. I read Trinity's words to her over the phone at 9 P.M. on a Friday night. She gasped. We sat in awe on either end of the telephone line, me looking at the message, Mary hearing it from my voice, hearing it freshly once again. I said, "Mary, I can't believe I never saw it. I can't believe I never realized it. Love is what it's all about, isn't it, Mary?"

240

Love was what everything had been about from the very beginning. From Gracie's life and death, to Julie hearing "God Bless Mary," to me opening my heart—it had all been about love. The love we gave and the love we received and the love that was surrounding us. The love that unites. The love that joins. The love that makes whole. The love that makes holy. The love that is our purpose. The love that is our Grace.

XXVII

GRACE

Grace is what happens when love and purpose come together into acceptance of ourselves as God created us and intended us to be. As we were created, we were perfect, as Grace Zuri Love was perfect. And all that is asked of us is that we return to what God created us and intended for us to be: ourselves.

As much as Julie, Mary, and I had spent the last quarter of the year searching for our purpose, we had, in a sense, missed it. For we were living our purpose.

Purpose is really about finding the self-love that allows us to see who we truly are, the self-love that enables us to look beyond ourselves with love, the self-love that allows us to act from love rather than judgment, to act from love instead of lack, to act from love instead of fear. It is about living the day-to-day ordinary life with love and grace and hope and connectedness and gratitude. It is about *trusting and sharing and growing.* It is about friendship and about extending friendship to all we meet in our day-to-day ordinary lives.

Purpose is the realization that the search for self and the search for God and the search for love are one and the same. That they are united as we are united. We had been living our purpose even when we hadn't realized it. And it was this unity of purpose that had brought us our connectedness. Unity of purpose is oneness. Unity of purpose is unity of will, is unity of mind, is unity of thought, is unity. This was the purpose that had sustained us through our beliefs in separate goals, separate journeys, separate selves.

Purpose is the realization that the search for self and the search for God and the search for love are, in their unity, about finding out who we are—in our unity. Not separately, not individually, not singularly, not alone. Our searches couldn't be separate for they had a united end. For there is only one purpose any of us can have and that is to *be who we are.* And none of us are who we are in a vacuum. Who I am is different from who Julie is. Different from who Mary is. We are different. But we are also the same.

We couldn't just concentrate on the different and find ourselves or God. We couldn't concentrate only on what was different and come to find love. We had to see the sameness, the equality, the unity, the oneness. We could each, by turning inward, find our uniqueness, but only by turning to each other, by sharing with each other, could we find our sameness. Both had to be found before we could be whole, before we could be united, before we could be who we truly are.

Being who we truly are is what allows us to meet life as it truly *is* rather than as we would have it be. It is saying "Thy will be done" rather than "I would have it be some other way." Being who we truly are is recognizing one united will. Is knowing that what God wants for us and what we want for ourselves and each other is the same— and that it is all there within our ordinary lives, just waiting for us. Waiting to be found in who we are.

Peace had told us:

Everything Gracie was was love. Pure love....

Grace, a being of love, had come into our lives with her own purpose, a purpose that was the *same* as ours. She came to *be who she was.* She came as love to give us *Love.* When Grace entered our lives, the ordinary and the extraordinary met. The human and the divine came together.

GRACE

Grace can enter your life too.

Out of the ashes life. Out of the darkness light. If it could happen to us, it could happen to anyone. This is our message.

Notes

1. Joseph Campbell with Bill Moyers, *The Power of Myth* (New York: Doubleday, 1991), 222.

2. Pat Rodegast and Judith Stanton, *Emmanuel's Book III: What Is an Angel Doing Here?* (New York: Bantam, 1994), 57.

3. Willis Harman and Howard Rheingold, *Higher Creativity: Liberating the Unconscious for Breakthrough Insights* (New York: Tarcher, 1984), 226.

4. James Hillman, *Insearch: Psychology and Religion* (Woodstock, Conn.: Spring Publications, 1994), 28.

ABOUT THE AUTHORS

Margaret Perron majored in English at the University of Minnesota where she won the Jean Keller-Bouvier Award for literary accomplishment. She has been a public relations director in the nonprofit sector and has worked in administration at the University of Minnesota while pursuing her interest in writing. She grew up in St. Paul, Minnesota, where she continues to find sustenance from her faith, her friends, and her family.

Julieanne Carver lives in Minneapolis with her husband, Kelly, and two children, Lucia and Peter. They own and operate a 10 bedroom Victorian guest residence. She holds a bsb from the Carlson School of Management at the University of Minnesota, enjoys music, quiet time (when she can get it!), and is working on several children's books.

Mary Kathryn Love lives in St. Paul, Minnesota, with her husband, stepdaughter, and four cats. She enjoys gardening and conversation, and has a deep appreciation for the quiet solitude that books and reading offer. She grew up in South America and attended high school and college in Minnesota. Love continues to write, having found this to be one of the aspects of life that contains her joy.

All three authors are currently program associates for the isp Executive Study Program at the University of Minnesota. The authors can be contacted through the web site of The Grace Foundation: http://www.gracezurilovefoundation.com

Hazelden Publishing and Education is a division of the Hazelden Foundation, a not-for-profit organization. Since 1949, Hazelden has been a leader in promoting the dignity and treatment of people afflicted with the disease of chemical dependency.

The mission of the foundation is to improve the quality of life for individuals, families, and communities by providing a national continuum of information, education, and recovery services that are widely accessible; to advance the field through research and training; and to improve our quality and effectiveness through continuous improvement and innovation.

Stemming from that, the mission of the publishing division is to provide quality information and support to people wherever they may be in their personal journey—from education and early intervention, through treatment and recovery, to personal and spiritual growth.

Although our treatment programs do not necessarily use everything Hazelden publishes, our bibliotherapeutic materials support our mission and the Twelve Step philosophy upon which it is based. We encourage your comments and feedback.

The headquarters of the Hazelden Foundation are in Center City, Minnesota. Additional treatment facilities are located in Chicago, Illinois; New York, New York; Plymouth, Minnesota; St. Paul, Minnesota; and West Palm Beach, Florida. At these sites, we provide a continuum of care for men and women of all ages. Our Plymouth facility is designed specifically for youth and families.

For more information on Hazelden, please call 1-800-257-7800. Or you may access our World Wide Web site on the Internet at http://www.hazelden.org.